Timeless Top 10 Travel Guides

New York City

New York City's Top 10 Hotel Districts, Shopping and Dining, Museums, Activities, Historical Sights, Nightlife, Top Things to do Off the Beaten Path, and Much More!

By Tess Downey

Foreword

New York City is one of the most popular tourist destinations in the world today. Everyone wants a slice of the big Apple. Strangely enough, not all slices are the same, but each one comes with a uniquely New York flavor.

Whether you come to New York City to go shopping, to indulge your taste buds, or to visit some of the most iconic landmarks in the world, there is something for everyone in the Great City. Christmas and New Year are always an event to see and be part of. The City contains some of the grandest architecture outside of Europe, and there are always magnificent events to see – whether concerts by some of the leading names in the music industry, home games in one of the City's sprawling sports stadiums, or a quiet stroll through appreciating some of humanity's best works of art in one of the City's numerous museums.

Try out some of their food – pizza is always on top of everybody's list of foods to try. Mingle with the locals, try riding the subway, or just simply enjoy the quiet serenity of New York City's Central Park. So strap on your walking shoes, make sure your camera is working well, and begin your explorations!

Table of Contents

Chapter 1: Introduction

New York City.

The City has been called by a lot of names: The Big Apple, The Concrete Jungle, The City That Never Sleeps. New York City is a beautiful, significant city, the financial, cultural and entertainment center of the United States, and its lingering shades of seediness and snatches of dark history only serves to add to its appeal.

There is no shortage of things to do in New York City. From some of the world-renowned iconic landmarks to oh-so recognizable landscapes in thousands of films and shows shot in New York City throughout the ages, there has always been some form of public consciousness of New York City in the world. Millions of immigrants have come to its shores in years past, looking for a better life – and having set up productive and lively communities within New York City itself, the resulting hot pot of cultures and ethnicities have only made the city richer and more interesting.

Even resident New Yorkers will tell you that you should visit New York City at least once in your lifetime. We hope that you do find at least one great reason within the pages of this book.

A Brief History of New York City

In order to fully appreciate the sights and sounds and the truly unique eclectic culture of New York City, it is a good idea to acquaint yourself with the City's history. While its written history began with Giovanni da Verrazano in 1524, the area of New York has always been a prime settlement location before the arrival of the Europeans – specifically the Lenape Native American people. The abundant waterways of the area were primary sources of food and trade, and sometimes even war. In fact, the Lenape's settlement had grown so much that an estimated 5,000 Lenape were already cultivating the fields, managing their resources, and the paths they created paved the way for what are now some of the main thoroughfares of New York City.

Because of the strategic location and importance of the area, New York City has had a long and important history to the development and growth of the country as a whole. Below is a brief timeline of the City's history, based mainly on written records after the arrival of the first European visitor to the lands:

- Giovanni da Verrazzano, in command of French ship La Dauphine, arrived in 1524. He met native Lenape, and sailed into Upper New York Bay, before finally leaving to continue his voyage. He subsequently named the area as *Nouvelle-Ancouleme* (New Angouleme) in honor of Francis I, the King of France.
- On September 2, 1609, Englishman Henry Hudson, in the employ of the Dutch East India Company, sailed through The Narrows and into Upper New York Bay. At the time, he was also looking for a westerly passage to Asia. He never did manage to reach Asia, but he noted an abundant beaver population – which led to the founding of Dutch trading colonies in the New World, as beaver pelts made for fashionable and lucrative business in Europe.
- A Dutch fur trading post was established in Lower Manhattan from 1624 – 1625. Fort Amsterdam was created in 1626. African slaves were brought to serve

as laborers, and the first walls of the city were built. This period was marked by a brutal war against the Native Americans which eventually resulted in a peace treaty on August 29, 1645.

- The colony was granted self-government in 1652, and New Amsterdam became incorporated as a city on February 2, 1653.
- England conquered the area in 1664, naming it "New York" after the Duke of York. It was later permanently ceded by the Dutch to the English in 1674.

- The British controlled New York from 1664 to 1783. They continued the Dutch practice of importing slaves from Africa – who served in various roles such as laborers, domestic servants and skilled trades.
- Agitation against British rule and for more autonomy had been underlying the New York settlement for some years, until given new impetus by the Stamp Act and other British measures. In 1765, the first organized resistance to British authority took place across the colonies. The Continental Army, led by General George Washington, was defeated in the Battle of Long Island in 1776. When their army later withdrew, British took control over Manhattan and the strategically important area of New York City. It

was the political and military center of the British in North America for the duration of the war.

- In 1783, George Washington returned to the city when the last of the British forces left. The Articles of Confederation were signed by Congress in 1789, and New York City became the first national capital of the United States. The first Congress sat at Federal Hall in Wall Street, as well as the first United States Supreme Court. This is where the United States Bill of Rights was drafted and ratified. New York City remained as the country's capital until 1790, when it was transferred to Philadelphia.
- The Erie Canal was opened in 1825, connecting the Atlantic port to the North American interior markets. A street grid system was developed to encompass all of Manhattan, and in 1842, water was piped to the city from a reservoir for the first time.
- A large influx of Irish immigrants arrived in New York City, driven by the Great Irish Famine from 1845-1850. During this time, public schools and the New York City Police Department were also established.
- New York City was home to many American literary figures during the 1830s. Central Park was later established in 1857 due to the lobbying of some of the city's business elite.

- Immigration continued, this time also bringing in immigrants from German provinces. The sympathies of the city were divided during the American Civil War from 1861-1865. The Draft Riots took place in 1863, due to the vast inequality among the population where wealthy men could simply pay to hire a substitute and thus avoid conscription. These riots eventually attacked the other elements of the City's population – including the blank New Yorkers with whom the Irish competed fiercely for work. The blacks mostly fled to areas outside of Manhattan such as Williamsburg, Brooklyn, and New Jersey, and the white working class became dominant.
- After the Civil War, the rate of immigration grew, and millions came to the United States, passing through the immigration processing center in New York City.
- The modern City of New York was formed in 1898, consolidating Brooklyn, Manhattan, and other outlying areas. Manhattan and the Bronx became two separate boroughs, and "Greater New York" was created. The first subway opened in 1904, bringing the different counties together, and New York City grew as a world industry and commercial center. Suburbs and skyscrapers were constructed. New York City dominated the nation in trade, finance, communication, and culture.

- The City also became a destination for internal immigrants, especially African Americans during the Great Migration from the rural South. Harlem Renaissance flourished in the 1920s. After World War I, trade routes were disrupted. The Immigration Restriction Acts limited immigration, and the Great Depression set in. The Gilded Age of Barons was at an end. And yet some of the city's landmark skyscrapers such as the Chrysler Building and the Empire State Building were built during the 1930s.
- Postwar economic boom was created by the return of World War II veterans and European immigration. Suburbs grew in Queens and Nassau County. A service economy overtook the shipbuilding and garment industries.
- From the 1960s to the early 1970s, the crime rate in New York City grew, and its reputation declined. Serial slayings by the Son of Sam struck fear into the hearts of many residents.
- In the 1980s, there was a rebirth of Wall Street. While crime and unemployment rates remained high, the City began to reclaim is position as the center of the financial industry. Neighborhood restoration projects began to breathe new life into New York City neighborhoods, and more businesses came to the city. The real estate industry boomed, and arts and culture

were integrated into the renovation of slowly eroding neighborhoods.

- A terrorist attack on September 11, 2001in which 2,606 people were killed in an attack on the twin towers of the World Trade Center. This reopened again as One World Trade Center on November 3, 2014. Despite these attacks, the City remained a major financial capital and tourist magnet, with some 40 million tourists visiting each year.

Chapter Two: Hotels and Accommodations

New York City is comprised of five boroughs: the Bronx, Brooklyn, Manhattan, Queens, and Staten Island. The quality of your visit to New York is influenced greatly by your needs and expectations, and how your choice of neighborhood and hotel meets those expectations.

There is literally something for everyone in New York City - the trick is knowing what you want and doing the required research to find the area that best suits your needs. Aside from your budget, a good location next to a subway station is important, and proximity to the places that you intend to visit during your stay.

Are you looking to visit museums, explore art galleries and maybe spend a night or two watching theatre? Or are you in New York to do some shopping and maybe have a gander at the best restaurants in the city? Maybe you are here to explore the City's history and marvel at the beautiful architecture and brownstone apartments that are still remarkably well-preserved. Street music and performers, pizza and hotdogs, world class sports, night clubs and jazz bars, or just the quiet and charm of a stroll along leafy avenues or beautiful neighborhoods and quiet family afternoons amidst verdant parks? It really depends on what you are looking for. Most New Yorkers will quickly tell you that there is no one "best" neighborhood to stay in, while just as quickly expressing great pride in their own particular neighborhood.

Be aware that the price ranges of hotels in New York City will be pretty steep compared to most of the rest of the country. Prime real estate commands high prices, and rents and hotel rates are steadily climbing due to the recent renovations, redevelopments, and gentrification of many of the City's oldest neighborhoods. What with millions of tourists flocking to New York City each year, the demand is high, and so rates are set accordingly.

Most of the popular tourist spots in New York City are located in Manhattan, and finding a good Manhattan hotel gives you easy access to many of these popular sights. And while parking yourself near Times Square can be both exciting, confusing and overwhelming, there are quieter neighborhoods in Manhattan that are also top choices for visiting tourists.

If you are on a very tight budget, you may consider finding alternatives outside of Manhattan. The other boroughs such as Queens and Brooklyn offer cheaper hotel rates, and equally beautiful sights and great restaurants. Due to the larger concentration of ethnically diverse cultures in these two areas, you can probably expect a richer and more authentic food adventure in these neighborhoods.

1. *Midtown Manhattan*

Midtown Manhattan extends lengthwise across the central portion of the island and borough of Manhattan, separating Lower Manhattan from Upper Manhattan. It is New York as has been seen in thousands of films – the largest commercial, entertainment, and media center in the United States, housing the tallest hotels and apartment towers, and is home to some of New York City's most iconic landmarks such as the Chrysler Building, Times Square, Broadway theatre, Fifth Avenue, the Empire State Building, the Grand Central Terminal, and the New York Public Library.

This is literally the "New York that never sleeps." If you want to find an area close to many of New York City's tourist destinations, this is a very convenient place to stay during your trip. This is assuming you don't mind being in the heart of the city that "never sleeps," or being in the middle of all the popular tourist destinations. Expect traffic and congestion, and expensive hotels and accommodations, including expensive restaurants.

Many people usually divide Midtown Manhattan into Midtown West and Midtown East. While Midtown West is where you'll find all the amazing sights, Midtown East is where you'll find all the grandest and most expensive hotels – in an area that is somewhat more residential. If you're not concerned about your budget and are in New York to "live it up" – the length of Midtown Manhattan can be a great area for you to find a good hotel to stay.

2. *Upper East Side and Upper West Side*

The Upper East Side and the Upper West Side are two different neighborhoods, though they are similar in some respects. Separated by Central Park, and located some distance from all the action of Midtown and downtown Manhattan, this is a quiet neighborhood with a more residential feel to it.

Both east and west feature beautiful brownstone townhouses, leafy avenues, and a good selection of fine dining, high end shopping, and museums galore to explore. These are the upscale neighborhoods of Manhattan, and hotel rooms can be a little pricey. But it is a charming area of New York City, and there is plenty of magnificent and beautiful architecture that only adds to the affluence, grandeur, and style. The area itself may even feel a bit familiar – chances are you have seen them featured in at least one movie or TV show in recent years.

These neighborhoods are some distance to the more vibrant areas of the city, and commuting to and from these areas can be a little tricky. But if what you're after is a quiet place to rest and relax, and a chance to just enjoy the more quiet and posh side of New York, this is a good area to park your heels.

3. *SoHo*

SoHo, or Soho, (i.e., "South of Houston Street") is located in Lower Manhattan, and is an area where you can find great restaurants, designer shopping boutiques and national and international chain store outlets. It is an attractive and historic neighborhood – and is home to the SoHo Cast Iron Historic District. There are still a good number of these beautiful and ornate buildings surviving today, and together with its cobblestone streets, certainly lend a unique kind of charm to the entire area.

Originally known as a place for artists who lived and worked in the lofts of what were once warehouses, there has been a recent influx of eclectic fashion boutiques and various chain outlets that now operate alongside the original art galleries. It is a diverse and interesting neighborhood, close to Chinatown, Little Italy, and Greenwich Village, though SoHo itself is pretty much high-end. Hotels here are also pretty expensive, and you're not likely to find budget or value accommodations. But it is certainly more quiet than the bustling Times Square district, and with major subway lines within easy walking distance, going elsewhere in New York should be easier.

4. *Chelsea*

It is said that many of the artists who relocated from SoHo found their new home in Chelsea. It is certainly the home of New York's contemporary art scene, with a great variety of art galleries and exhibits to explore. Chelsea is also considered the hub of New York's gay culture, and affords the visitor a vibrant nightlife, but without the noise and traffic of Times Square.

Chelsea is also friendlier to the budget-conscious tourist, providing a good selection of accommodations from high-end to something a bit more moderate. There are nearby places where you can immerse yourself in theater and opera, great dining places, and a variety of shopping places such as Madison Square Garden, Union Square, and of course, Chelsea Market.

Chelsea also features the Chelsea historic district – so listed in 1971. This includes a development consisting of Greek Revival and Italianate row houses from the 18th century estate of Captain Thomas Clarke. It was envisioned to be a first-class residential area, but though it remained middle class to this day, these 2-3 story row houses certainly lend character and beauty to this already interesting neighborhood.

5. *Lower Manhattan*

Lower Manhattan is Downtown Manhattan, and is the city's center for business, culture, and government. It is located at the southernmost tip of the island of Manhattan, and it is where, it can be said, the city of New York first began.

Lower Manhattan includes the Financial District and Wall Street, the New York Stock Exchange, various government offices such as City Hall, and the World Trade Center site. There is also Chinatown, the South Street Seaport, the Brooklyn Bridge, some pretty amazing skyscrapers, and the embarkation point for ferries to Staten Island, Liberty Island, and Ellis Island.

Because this area caters more to businessmen and businesswomen, the rates can get pretty steep, although you can probably find savings if you stay over on a weekend or non-business days. It can be quiet during the night, though there are some good bars, restaurants, and places to shop. The streets are also pretty narrow – a throwback to the footpaths and canals of the original settlements in the area. This is well-situated for a visitor with business to attend to in the area, with many entertainment spots to relax and unwind.

6. *Flatiron District*

Bounded by Union Square on one end and Gramercy Park on the other, New York City's Flatiron District is quintessential and classic New York. The name of the district derives from the Flatiron Building at 23rd Street, Broadway and Fifth Avenue – one of the original New York skyscrapers.

This is a beautiful neighborhood where charming historic buildings are more prominent than skyscrapers. The area is also notable for its great restaurants, markets, and an active street life. The Ladies' Mile Historic District is also located here – one of the prime shopping destinations of the affluent at the end of the 19th century. While most of those shops and department stores have since moved uptown, the buildings they used to occupy still remain, and have since been renovated and are now occupied by smaller, though no less interesting shops and stores.

Also on the plus side, Union Square has a subway hub that can pretty much bring you everywhere else in New York. And aside from the magnificent restaurants and shopping, there are also great lodging choices here.

This neighborhood is pretty upscale too, though, and rooms will not be cheap. But it is centrally located with easy access to other tourist spots via subway.

7. *Lower East Side*

The Lower East Side is another interesting place to stay, although recent developments and gentrification has increased the price range of hotels in this area although one can still find a few decent places for a more reasonable price.

This is a vibrant neighborhood in an edgy kind of way – a thriving street life, eclectic restaurants, fashionable bistros, and hip clubs. When you look around, you'll find blocks of tenement buildings that once housed the immigrant population of New York, and there are still distinct traces left of the ethnically diverse lower class working neighborhood that once lived there: from Irish, Italians, Poles, Ukrainians, Germans, and Jewish immigrants, among others.

Most of the original residents have moved on, though the Chinese population which spilled over from nearby Chinatown are now the dominant immigrant group. And with a new wave of young urban professionals moving in, the neighborhood has since been revitalized and is now a prime real estate market. It's a good place to stay if you want to immerse yourself in diverse cultures, while at the same time looking to enjoy the New York night scene. On the other hand, it is some distance from the more renowned tourist areas of New York, though multiple subway stations in the neighborhood should simplify the dilemma of getting around the rest of Manhattan.

8. Greenwich Village

Greenwich Village is also often referred to as "West Village," or simply "the Village." This is primarily a residential area, and is known for its artistic and literary community, and traces of its bohemian roots are still pretty evident . Landmarks of the neighborhood include NYU and Washington Square Park, charming brownstones, narrow streets, and intimate dining spots. It is also famously known for being the main setting of the "Friends" TV show.

It is one of the more laid-back areas of Manhattan, without all the glitz and glamour of the more luxurious neighborhoods. There are a good selection of more affordable rooms here, in a neighborhood that is relatively quiet without being too quiet. There are great bars to choose from, intimate restaurants, and the rather grungy street art and indie music scene makes it more charmingly romantic rather than fast paced or opulent.

9. *Brooklyn*

Lying along the southwestern end of Long Island, Brooklyn is the second largest of the boroughs of New York in terms of land area. It also has a rich and engaging history, culture, and dynamic growth all its own, and quite distinct from the more dominant Manhattan borough. It is still a melting pot of diverse cultures and ethnicities which only serve to make Brooklyn rich and exciting in a very cosmopolitan sort of way.

The tourist will find hotel rates here relatively cheaper compared to Manhattan price ranges, and while you may be far from the action if you opt to stay in Brooklyn, the borough itself is well served by various transportation modes such as the subway, bus lines, cabs, commuter railway stations, and a ferry system. On the other hand, Brooklyn has amazing sights and tourist spots which are well-worth checking out, too - not to mention amazing restaurants and locally flavored cuisine. This is also a great place to stay if you're aiming to enjoy a cruise, as Brooklyn has long been a major shipping port, and is now central to New York City's growing cruise industry.

10. Queens

Adjacent to the borough of Brooklyn, and located towards the southwestern end of Long Island, Queens encompasses the largest land area among New York City's five boroughs. It is also considered to be the most ethnically diverse urban area in the world.

If making a good round of local restaurants and food tripping is a big part of your visit to New York, then this is perhaps the best place for you to stay as Queens is well known for its diverse and amazing range of international cuisine.

Queens is also known for the world-class sporting events it offers enterprising tourists, beautiful parks and museums, and amazing beaches on Rockaway Beach.

While the neighborhood offers visitors a comparatively quiet New York visit (as opposed to a visit to the Manhattan hotspots), there are those who say that the diversity and rich cultural experience of Queens is what quintessential New York is all about.

Chapter Three: Shop and Dine in New York City

Food is practically a culture in New York City, and so is the shopping. Many tourists who come to the City do so for either or both, and New York City hardly disappoints. There are shops and boutiques and discount stores practically in every borough in New York, and dining choices range from street food to pizza to cafés and fine dining. The different cultures and ethnicities that now make up a substantial population of New York City have only served to enliven these aspects, and your options for culinary specialties and shopping bazaars can pretty much take you all over the world, if you know where to look.

The recent gentrification of New York City has had its own effect too – revitalizing neighborhoods, or seeing the mass movement of communities to different areas. In most instances, this does mean a rise in price ranges, so be prepared. Check out the areas that are within your price range – or you can simply window shop in the more affluent areas if you wish. Don't forget to enjoy the culture, grandeur and diversity as you go around the City.

1. *Rockefeller Center*

A premier shopping and dining location, Rockefeller Center is a national historic landmark located in the heart of Midtown Manhattan. It is a large complex of 19 high-rise commercial buildings located between 48th and 51st streets, commissioned by the Rockefeller family.

Originally, John D. Rockefeller intended the area for an opera house, but after the stock market crash of 1929 and continuous delays, Rockefeller was forced to abandon the original plans and move ahead as sole financier of one of the largest private building project in modern times.

The original opera house project was not included, and instead there arose 14 buildings in the Art Deco Style. Rockefeller Center opened in 1939. For a time, it also served as the base of U.S. operations of British Intelligence and

British Security Coordination during the war, with Room 3603 the principal operations center for Allied Intelligence.

At present, Rockefeller Center is composed of two building complexes: the original 1930s 14 Art Deco office buildings, with an additional building across 51st Street that was later built in 1947. The second is a set of four towers along the west side of the Avenue of the Americas. At the heart of Rockefeller Center is 30 Rockefeller Plaza, which lies under the shadow of 30 Rockefeller Center, also called Comcast Building, and sometimes 30 Rock. The Lower Plaza is where the annual famed Rockefeller Center Christmas Tree is lit, and also the popular ice skating rink. At the top of 30 Rock is the Center's observation deck, which gives visitors an amazing 360-degree panoramic view of New York City.

Rockefeller Center is also home to Radio City Music Hall, or Radio City, with an interior that boasts the world's greatest example of Art Deco design, and seats 6,000 people. The Center itself is sometimes referred to simply as "Radio City."

For those looking to shop and dine, there is an underground pedestrian passage that runs from 47th to 51st street, from Fifth Avenue to Seventh Avenue. Access can be had through any of six landmark buildings, elevators and restaurants surrounding the skating rink. This passage is filled with shops and restaurants for the enterprising tourist.

Over all, Rockefeller Center has over 100 unique fashion, gifts and souvenir shops, and just as many and as varied restaurants where you can grab a quick lunch, have a cocktail, or have an amazing fine dining experience.

2. *Fifth Avenue*

Fifth Avenue has long been acclaimed as one of New York City's premier shopping destinations. It starts just north of Washington Square, all the way up to 143rd street in Harlem. It features some of the most prestigious shops around – and is considered among the most expensive shopping streets in the world.

The high status of Fifth Avenue was established early on – since 1862 - as the home of New York City's social elite when Caroline Schermerhorn moved in and the Waldorf-Astor Hotel was established. It was largely a residential district to begin with. The first commercial building was built here only in 1906, with the establishment of B. Altman and Company. Since then, it has become the fashion destination of high end shoppers and the upscale stores that catered to them. Penthouses in the buildings along Fifth Avenue have been called the "most coveted real estate" by Forbes magazine in 2008.

Fabulous shopping destinations include Saks Fifth Avenue, Bergdorf-Goodman, Louis Vuitton, Prada, Gucci, Ferragamo, Gucci, Emanuel Ungaro, Bottega Veneta, Harry Winston, Nike, Emilio Pucci, Zara, Ralph Lauren, and Lacoste, among others. There is also Harry Winsdon, Bulgari, Cartier, Tiffany's, and Van Cleef and Arpels for jewelry, Bergdorf Men and the Yankees Clubhouse Shop that caters to men, as well as the Microsoft Store and the famous underground Apple Store.

In fact, Fifth Avenue can be a one-place stop for a New York visit – as it is also home to many of the city's notable landmarks such as the Empire State Building, the Flatiron Building, New York Public Library, Rockefeller Center, St. Patrick's Cathedral, and a wonderful selection of amazing museums along Museum Mile.

Famished after all that shopping? Fifth Avenue offers more than enough spots to satisfy your gastronomic cravings. From street foods like The Famous Halal Guys, Angelo's Pizza, Margon, Café Cello, and Uncle Gussy's, to international cuisine like Japanese Katsu-Hama, Turkish food at Akdeniz, Burger Joint, or Chinese at Xi-an Famous Foods, and something a bit more fancy at fine dining restaurants such as Smith & Wollensky, La Grenouille, and db Bistro Moderne, among others. There's lots more to explore.

3. *South Street Seaport*

If you are hankering for something a bit more unique in your shopping and dining experiences, look no further than the South Street Seaport.

Located between Brooklyn Bridge and Wall Street, this historic district in Lower Manhattan not only offers a great variety of shopping and dining options, there are also seasonal entertainment, rich cultural activities, harbor cruises, and much more.

Relive the heyday of what was once the busiest port in America. This is the location of the largest concentration of restored early 19th century commercial buildings in America. Other notable historical points of interest are the Titanic Memorial Lighthouse, the former Fulton Fish Market, historic ships – five of which are docked at least semi-permanently, including the United States Lightship LV-87 (1908), Lettie G. Howard (1893), Pioneer (1885), W.O. Decker (1930), and Wavertree (1885). The port also offers visitors a wonderful view of the Brooklyn Bridge. You can also visit the South Street Seaport Museum to learn more about the history of the port. The area around the museum is a great place to go for a stroll, too, and you can enjoy the beautiful 18th and 19th century buildings and homes that are part of the historic district. At Schermerhorn Row, a row of twelve early 19th century warehouses, are a diverse range of restaurants, shops and galleries to explore.

This is a great place to bring the kids to, and there are more than enough shopping and dining options to satisfy your hunger and shopping cravings. Pier 17 is probably the most famous – a shopping mall that carried everything while providing a great view of the Brooklyn Bridge. It was demolished in 2014, though Pier 17 is expected to reopen again in 2017, this time as a brand new glass complex.

Every with Pier 17 currently out of commission, however, there are other places to explore. Try out Lee Lee's Forest, Browne & Co. Stationers, Modabox, Seaport Studios, D.U.O. GEAR, and Puma City. Prices are certainly more affordable compared to the affluent shopping districts of Manhattan, but there is surely no shortage of diversity and interesting things to see. And for something to eat, try out some of the crowd favorites such as Tabasco Grill, Made Fresh Daily, Acqua, and MarkJoseph Steakhouse.

4. *Nolita and Little Italy*

Little Italy may not be what it used to be – ever since the end of World War II, the original immigrant residents have been moving out and moving on to other neighborhoods in New York, primarily Brooklyn, Staten

Island, Eastern Long Island, and even as far as New Jersey. Some residents could simply no longer afford the rising rents and real estate prices, or of those who achieved quick financial prosperity, they moved out of their cramped apartments and into more spacious surroundings elsewhere. The one-time dominance of Italians in Little Italy is simply no longer true.

Little Italy – and Nolita (or North of Little Italy), have lately gone through a revival of sorts, with the influx of new business in the area. Nolita has become one of New York City's hottest shopping districts, including the flagship of James Jebba's Supreme Beings that caters to the skateboarding culture; McNally Jackson and the Housing Works Bookstore Café for an excellent selection of used books and a convenient café for book lovers; or for those looking to shop for fashion, a stroll along Elizabeth Street will provide you with plenty of options. Also check out Opening Ceremony on Howard Street and Amarcord on Lafayette for something a bit more eclectic. Shopping for ingredients? Try Alleva Dairy or Di Palo.

And yes, Italian restaurants are still very much evident in this area, with some longtime restauranteurs such as Piemonte Ravioli, De Gennaro Restaurant, Ferrara Bakery & Café, Lombardi's Pizza, and Pomodoro Rsitorante & Pizzeria. There's also a bunch of cafés, bars, and watering holes to go for a shot of caffeine or a nightcap, such as La

Colombe, Gimme! Coffee, LaSweet & Vicious, La Esquina, and Inga.

5. *Macy's Herald Square*

Macy's is a veritable institution when it comes to shopping. It is the world's largest department store – with an area of 2.2 million square feet and 11 floors, Macy's flagship at Herald Square in Manhattan has been in operation since it first opened in 1924. It has been standing on its current site for some 115 years now, and has been added to the National Register of Historic Placed and recognized as a National Historic Landmark in 1879.

It all started with R.H. Macy Dry Goods owned by Rowland Hussey Macy from Massachussetts. He expanded as the business grew, eventually moving to the elite "Ladies' Mile" shopping district.

Long after Macy and his partners had died, the store was acquired by brothers Isidor and Nathan Straus, who decided to make the move uptown to Herald Square. Here, there was progressive growth of the store, and the Palladian façade of the original building has been built upon and updated with the purchase of nearby properties to add to the store. To this day, some of its original wooden escalators are still in operation.

Macy's has since become an iconic part of New York City, and it houses numerous stores, restaurants, and eateries. This large department store caters to everyone, and it offers customers so much variety in product that the difficulty is more in choosing than in finding. Also quite convenient to have restaurants in the same building when you feel your stomach growling after a hard day of shopping – assuming you can think of its vast area as "one building" – which yes, it is.

6. *Madison Avenue*

Madison Avenue is the place to go for some luxurious shopping. Located in Manhattan, and stretching from Madison Square (from which its name derives) all the way to 142nd street.

Madison Avenue has its roots in the advertising industry – and since the 1920s, has been the major location of most major advertising firms in New York City. The identification had become so strong that Madison Avenue was almost synonymous to advertising for most Americans. Today, however, only a few advertising agencies remain on Madison Avenue – most have moved to different locations, though the connection to Madison Avenue is still pretty strong in the industry.

Today, Madison Avenue has become associated with luxurious shopping, and many retail brands are located here including Calvin Klein, Roberto Cavalli, Davidoff, Tom Ford, Giorgio Armani, Ralph Lauren, Victoria's Secret, Barney's New York, Prada, Vera Wang and a lot more.

Fine shopping should definitely be followed by stylish dining, and Madison Avenue offers a good choice of high-end restaurants such as the Carlyle Restaurant. There is also Peacock Alley and Gilt NY, with more budget-conscious alternatives such as S Dynasty and the Met Grill.

7. *Bedford Avenue Williamsburg*

Plenty of budget-friendly options are available in Williamsburg's Bedford Avenue – Brooklyn's longest street that stretches from Manhattan Avenue in Greenpoint to Sheepshead Bay. Bedford Avenue itself literally passes through a good diversity of New York City's cultural and ethnic communities, including African American, American, Hasidic, Hispanic, Russian, and Polish neighborhoods. You can therefore expect a good diversity of hip boutiques, record stores, street stalls, thrift shops, and vintage emporiums.

A good place to go if you're looking for something different, hip, or vintage without having to be too conscious of your budget.

If you want to add a little history to your shopping and dining jaunt, try the Studebaker Building and the 23rd Regiment Armory.

8. *Chelsea Market*

Located in the Chelsea neighborhood of Manhattan, and interestingly housed in the same site that once served as the Nabisco Biscuit Company factory complex where, it is said, the Oreo cookie was invented, Chelsea Market is one of the best indoor food halls in the world. And to make it even more interesting, the High Line actually passes straight through the building on the 10th Avenue side.

Can you "shop for food?" You sure can. Chelsea Market attracts about 6 million visitors each year. Food certainly draws a crowd. Here, you can purchase anything from soup to nuts, cheese to cheesecake, whether fresh ingredients or unique dishes. There are more than 35 vendors offering a great variety of great food. Try out some of their anchor stores such as Chelsea Market Baskets, Manhattan Fruit Exchange, Anthropologie, Ruth's Bakery, Buddakan restaurant, Amy's Bead, Chelsea Wine Vault, and The Green Table, among others. And to further bolster the locality's expertise on food – the Chelsea Market is also home to the Food Network by "Iron Chef" Masaharu Morimoto.

9. *Orchard Street Shopping District, Lower East Side*

Orchard Street on the Lower East Side was a center of immigrant culture – first being known as Little Germany, and then later as a Jewish enclave. The street is also essentially known as the heart of the Lower East Side – and was known for its discount shopping. Some of the oldest shops are still there: clothing and luggage stores such as Altman Luggage, A.W. Kaufman, M. Katz and Sons, Moscot Eyewear, Zarin Fabrics, and Cohen's Fashion Optical. Due to increasing gentrification, however, trendy and hip boutiques are becoming established alongside these older businesses, thus drawing in a more diversified crowd. Look out for Dressing Room, Edith Machinist, Grit N Glory, Rainbow Apparel, By Robert James, and The Cast, among many others.

Each Sunday, Orchard Street is closed to vehicular traffic, and the street becomes a virtual pedestrian mall. Sundays would be a great time to take a stroll down Orchard Street and peruse the wares of the merchants who bring tables outside their shops to hawk their wares, so to speak.

This would also be a good time to join the friendly neighborhood community for a bite or a drink after all that shopping. And because of the cultural diversity of the neighborhood, you can expect some excitement and uniqueness in the culinary fare in this area, too! There's more than enough choices for something to dine on – whether you are looking for a light snack or something more filling. Try out Tiny Fork, Alegre, Todd's Mill, Mi Casa Es Su Casa, Black Tree, Russ & Daughters Café, Café Katja, Fung Tu, and Contra, among many others.

10. Brooklyn Flea

If what you're looking for include vintage clothing, repurposed furniture, antiques, arts and crafts, jewelry, and local food, then head over to the Brooklyn Flea Market, where there will surely be enough to satisfy your shopping needs.

Often held in two locations: Fort Greene and the waterfront near Pearl Plaza, Brooklyn Flea has also recently launched Smorgasborg, located near the waterfront, which people have called a festival for food. The diversity is amazing – from handmade food to clean and sterile stalls.

Try your taste buds at Bocata, Bon Chovie, Meat Hook, Cemita's, Shorty Tang & Sons, or the Brooklyn Oyster

Party. The Brooklyn Flea Market caters to some 4-5 thousand people daily. That is a lot of mouths to feed. Thankfully, the local cuisine experts are more than up to the task.

Chapter Four: A Feast For The Eyes

Begin your trip through New York City by a tour of some of the biggest museums in the country.

New York City has long been the center of artistic and cultural movements and historical preservation – what with millions of art galleries and museums scattered throughout the five boroughs, you simply cannot visit New York without visiting some of the best-loved museums of all. Marvel at works of art from all over the world – beautifully rendered paintings and sculptures by some of the finest masters, or treat yourself to edgy and more modern pieces that provoke as well as inspire. Or take a tour through the history of New York and the natural world through some of the carefully preserved pieces of history, relics and memorabilia lovingly preserved and presented within awe-inspiring buildings and façades that are works of art all their own.

Certainly one of the best, most enjoyable and inspirational ways of learning about art, history and culture is by walking through actual representations of human artistic expressions, visually documented histories, and the stories that they tell. Bring your family or go alone, and walk through the halls and galleries of some of the finest museums in New York City.

1. The Metropolitan Museum of Art

The largest art museum in the United States, the Metropolitan Museum of Art, also known as "the Met," is one of the most visited art museums in the world. It is located along the eastern edge of Central Park, and features a permanent collection of over three million works – from classical antiquity, ancient Egypt, works from European masters in painting and sculpture, and American modern art, among others, all curated by seventeen separate and specialized departments.

One of the Met's most popular collections feature the Department of Arms and Armor. There are also works of art from the Ancient Near East, Asia, Africa, the Americas, and Oceania. Its American wing offers visitors a view of some of America's finest paintings, sculptures and decorative arts.

The Met was founded in 1870 by a group of businessmen, financiers, and the leading artists and thinkers of their day. It opened for the first time in February 20, 1872, in its original location on Fifth Avenue. As the museum's collection grew, however, more space was needed, and it eventually found its new and present home in a specially designed building near Central Park. Today, the Met also includes the Met Cloisters in Fort Tryon Park, and the Met Breuer in the Upper East Side, the latter of which only opened in March 2016.

The Met is generally open daily (except for holidays) and charges a general admission of $25, with discounts for seniors and students. Children and New York public school students accompanied by adults are allowed inside for free.

2. *The Met Cloisters*

The Cloisters is part of the Metropolitan Museum of Art, thus it is sometimes referred to as the Met Cloisters. It is located in Fort Tryon in Upper Manhattan, and specializes in a collection of European medieval architecture, sculpture, and arts.

The history of the Cloisters Museum began with the private collection of George Grey Barnard, which was subsequently acquired by philanthropist John D. Rockefeller, Jr. Rockefeller expanded the collection, and later on purchased land at Washington Heights, contracting the architectural design for the distinctive building that now stands there and is known as the Cloisters Museum.

The design of the building incorporates parts from four medieval cloistered abbeys from France: the Cuxa, Bonnefort, Trie, and Saint-Guilhem cloisters. These were disassembled, shipped, and reconstructed again in New York City, building from these parts a cohesive whole in the very construction of the Cloisters. The architectural elements of the building itself is part of the collection – as well as stained glass, manuscripts, and various medieval works of art. The Museum's importance extends to the grounds and one of the most important specialized gardens in the world: containing over 250 genera of plants, herbs, flowers and trees, most of which are medieval species. The entire collection is, in fact, intended to recreate and reproduce French medieval and monastic life.

A visit to the Cloisters is a breathtaking and instructive tour that will literally transport you to another age and another world. To further educate tourists as to what they are seeing, the museum frequently holds free gallery talks in which visitors are enlightened about medieval monastery life. They also hold an Annual Medieval Festival on the second of October where you can actually "live" in medieval times – or at least, be part of a recreated market town that is bustling with food and drinks and performers, where vendors and guests all wear appropriate costumes and join in the fun. The best part of all is that it's all free!

3. *American Museum of Natural History*

The American Museum of Natural History is found in the Upper West Side of Manhattan, and is actually an extensive complex of 28 interconnected buildings and containing 45 permanent exhibition halls. There are over 33 million specimens of plants, animals, fossils, minerals, rocks, human remains, meteorites, and artifacts in the museum's extensive collection, although only a small portion of this can be displayed at any given time. An entire day might not even be enough to go through the entire museum's displays.

This is a great place to bring the kids and the entire family. Join the other visitors on free tours that come with admission. Some of its more popular attractions include the dinosaur wing, a life-size model of a blue whale in the Milstein Hall, and the museum even has a planetarium and an IMAX theater. It's a great place to recapture one's interest and sense of wonder in the natural world. Tired from all those miles of exhibits and displays? The Museum also offers plenty of places where you can eat, or shop and buy souvenirs.

4. *The Lower East Side Tenement Museum*

The Lower East Side Tenement Museum is an actual five-story brick tenement building that used to be home to around 7,000 people of different ethinicities from over 20 nations. The tenement was in operation from between 1863 to 1935, and is now considered a National Historic Site.

Perhaps more than magnificent art works or fashionable displays, this is a museum that presents the human condition as it actually was. It is intended to promote tolerance by providing the visitor with a very close look at the immigrant experience.

The building used to be owned by Prussian Lukas Glockner, and was modified several times in order to conform with the city's housing laws. In 1935, however, the owner elected to evict the residents instead of initiating continued modifications. Only the basement and stoop-level storefronts were left open, while the upper floors were sealed. In 1988, the Tenement Museum was founded.

The exhibits and displays are presented as a kind of time capsule to show visitors the conditions of the lives of its residents, as well as to provide a lesson on housing conditions. There are walking tours and readings offered, and you can view the actual living conditions of the immigrants in the past. Walking through the cramped living spaces of what seems like actual people and families living in them can transport you to a whole new different time and reality.

5. *Museum of Modern Art (MoMA)*

Looking for something a bit more edgy than the usual classical art? Try something modern. The Museum of Modern Art or MoMA features one of the largest museums of modern art in the world today. It is located centrally in Midtown Manhattan, between Fifth and Sixth Avenues, and is a wonderfully interesting and exhilarating way to spend a New York City afternoon.

The MoMA was the brainchild of Abby Aldrich Rockefeller, wife of John D. Rockefeller, Jr., and two of her friends. They were collectively known as "the daring ladies" or "the adamantine ladies," and the MoMA was the first of its kind to exhibit modernist art in Manhattan. It began in rented galleries at the twelfth floor of the Heckscher

Building in 1929, moving to several other locations before moving to its present location in the Time-Life Building in Rockefeller Center in 1939. This was subsequently redesigned and renovated to accommodate a continuously expanding collection.

Some of its notable collections include an impressive collection of well-known favorites by Van Gogh, Picasso, Monet, Cezanne, Salvador Dali, Matisse, and Henri Rousseau, among others. The Museum also has an impressive art photography collection, as well as more than 4 million film stills.

While admission to the MoMA is set at $20, entry at Fridays after 4pm is free, and New York collge students are also allowed free admission to the museum.

6. *Frick Collection*

In the Upper East Side of Manhattan in New York City is the Henry Clay Frick House, a museum containing a portion of the private collection of coke and steel industrialist Henry Clay, which house and its contents as a public museum. The house was not converted into a public museum, however, until after the death of his widow Adelaide Howards Childs Frick, who retained the right of residence in the mansion until her death in 1931.

The Frick Collection in New York is actually part of the Frick At & Historical Center, which also includes a considerable collection in Frick's former Clayton residence in Pittsburgh, as well as a number of works that were donated by his daughter and heiresss to the Frick Fine Arts Building in the University of Pittsburgh. The Manhattan Building itself underwent enlargement and some renovation in order to make it a viable public institution. It opened to the public in 1977, and the collection itself was since expanded to include other artworks since acquired by his surviving daughter Helen.

In the museum's six galleries, the Frick collection encompasses amazing, high quality items such as Limoges enamels, English 18th century portraits, French 18th century paintings and furniture, Chinese porcelain, Italian paintings and bronzes, and Dutch 17th century works of art – created by some of the finest European masters such as Rembrandt, Giovanni Bellini, El Greco, Johannes Vermeer, and Joshua Reynolds among others. The Frick Collection is an amazing gathering of some of the finest works of art in human history.

7. The National 9/11 Memorial & Museum

For a more recent exploration of New York City's history, and what is likely to prove an emotional experience to many – one can visit the September 11 Memorial & Museum. This was founded to commemorate the September 11, 2001 attacks, where 2,977 people died, as well as the bombing of the World Trade Center, in which six persons were killed.

Located at the site of the former site of the Twin Towers, the 9/11 Memorial and Museum is on an 8 acre park, and was designed to be amidst a forest of trees, with two square pools at the center, or the "footprints" or the underground foundations of the Twin Towers. The names of the victims of the attacks are inscribed on 76 bronze plates attached to the parapets surrounding the waterfalls. This was based on the winning design "Reflecting Absence" by Michael Arad and Peter Walker.

The Memorial was opened to the public on September 12, 2011, while the Museum was opened to the public on May 21, 2014. Some three months after the memorial was opened, it had been visited by a record of over a million people, while some 42,000 people visited the Museum within five days after it opened.. Private tours are also offered by the 9/11 Tribute Center, which is hosted by family members of the victims, the responders, and survivors.

Featured in the Memorial are the Survivor Tree and the Survivor Staircase. The Museum, on the other hand, contains a vast collection of exhibits such as images, oral histories of those who were affected by the tragedy, and other artifacts from Ground Zero. The entire museum is intended to "evoke memories without additional distress."

8. Museum of the City of New York

The Museum of the City of New York is a good place to start if you're a relative stranger to NYC, including its past and present historical contexts. Knowing something about the city's history, origins, and evolution is a great way to enrich the r.est of your trip, and this museum's intention is to preserve and present the history of everything about New York City.

The MCNY is located along Fifth Avenue, in the Upper East neighborhood of Manhattan, just across from Central Park. It stands at the northern end of what is commonly known as the Museum Mile section of Fifth Avenue. The Museum building was designated a New York City landmark in 1967.

The museum originated from a successful exhibit of "Old New York in 1926. Today, its collections span over 1.5 million items – various paintings, objects, prints, photographs, rare book and manuscripts, and even toys, that relate in one way or another to the history of New York City and its residents. Some of its notable exhibits feature displays revolving around theater performances in New York, professional baseball, and social activitism.

The Museum exhibits capture the essence of the "personality" of New York – from architecture, urban landscapes, cultures, peoples, sights and sounds, and events that have made New York City what it is today.

9. *Morgan Library & Museum*

Ork, began

This seemingly small and unassuming Museum in Murray Hill in Manhattan, New York, is both a museum and a research center. Formerly known as the Pierpoint Morgan Library – it began from the private library of American banker and financier J.P Morgan, and was made a public institution by his son, John Pierpoint Morgan, in 1924, in accordance with his father's will. In 1966, it was designated a New York City landmark, and that same year was declared a National Historic Landmark.

If you love books, you'll be amazed at some of the rare and precious manuscripts that are part of this museum's collection, including illuminated manuscripts, metalwork covers of the Lindau Gospels, the Morgan Bible, Morgan Black Hours, Codex Glazier, and even medieval artworks such as the Stavelot Triptych. Original manuscipts of various authors are also housed here, including some by Sir Walter Scott and Honore de Balzac, and even scraps of paper on which Bob Dylan wrote down some of his famous songs such as "Blowin' in the Wind" and "It Ain't Me, Babe."

There are prints and drawings from major European artists, medieval liturgical objects, and autographed and annotated libretti and scores from composers such as Beethoven, Brahms and Chopin. The magnitude of the collection in this Museum is carefully kept in a richly decorated and beautiful interior. As the collection grew, the original McKim Building underwent renovations and expansion, and now includes an annex building, a modernist entrance building, and even a large performance hall where concerts are held.

10.Museum at Eldridge Street

Located in Manhattan's Chinatown neighborhood, the Eldridge Street Synagogue was reopened as a museum in December 2, 2007 as Museum at Eldridge Street.

Designated as a National Historic Landmark, the Eldridge Street Synagogue was first built in 1887, and is one of the first synagogues to be built in the United States by

Easter European Jews. It is a beautiful building and easily inspired the admiration of many for its imposing Moorish Revival façade, a 70 foot high vaulted ceiling, and magnificent stained-glass rose windows.

It was actively in use as a place for religious services throughout the 1920s, and also served as a place of refuge and acculturation for new Jewish Americans. But in the next fifty years, membership dwindled. People moved to other areas, and the Great Depression set in. Beset by disrepair and with not enough members left, the sanctuary was cordoned off in the 1950s.

Restoration and renovation of the Eldridge Synagogue began on December of 2007, and went on for the next 20 years. When renovations were finished, it was reopened to the public as the Museum at Eldridge Street, offering exhibits, tours and displays that feature American Jewish history, including a history of the Lower East Side and the immigration experience. Even today, the synagogue is awe-inspiring in its magnificence – both in the interior of the sanctuary and the exterior Victorian façade. It also throws into greater context the lives of the original Jewish immigrants, their way of life, and the impact that the Eldridge Synagogue must have had on their faith, hopes and dreams. Today, the museum welcomes some 15,000 to 20,000 visitors each year.

Chapter Five: Seeing the Past in New York City's Present

From its very beginnings, the importance of New York City as a strategic harbor and center for economic trade has been unmatched. The history of New York is, in fact, closely tied with the growth of the country itself – from its original Native American inhabitants, to the European settlers, the British conquest and the revolution, and finally a strong stand for independence and autonomy. New York City has been the destination for immigrants to the United States, and it also saw the economic benefits, as well as the abolition, of slavery. Even though it is no longer the capital of the United States, nobody could deny New York City's preeminent role as a financial, business, and cultural center in the country and the world.

While New York City did undergo decline during its long history, it has recently made the move towards restoration and renovation of many of the notable architecture and neighborhoods in the City. Crime does still exist, but the rates have severely declined from what it was in the 60s-70s. The gentrification process is dusting off and once again bringing to light some of the more famous New York City landmarks that have characterized its rich and colorful past. It is still a rich cultural epicenter – a center of arts and culture, and a financial and business center.

Millions of people visit New York City each year. While you're here, don't forget to check out some of the City's notable historical landmarks and sights. They can still give us a significant glimpse of turbulent past of this world-famous Metropolis.

1. *Statue of Liberty*

Perhaps no other New York monument is more recognizable than Lady Liberty, who stands with her beacon held high on Liberty Island at the entrance of New York

Harbor, and has welcomed millions of immigrants to the United States since it was first inaugurated in 1886.

The idea for this monument began with Édouard René de Laboulaye, the president of the French Anti-Slavery Society, and sculptor Frédéric Bartholdi, a Union supporter during the American Civil War. It was a gift intended to honor the Union victory and to celebrate the common ideals of freedom and democracy. It was hoped that the French people would also be inspired to fight for their own democracy even under the rule of a repressive monarchy under Napoleon III.

While the idea may have begun sometime in 1865 to 1870, it wasn't until 1871 that action was begun on the idea – when Bartholdi came to the United States, carrying letters of introduction from Laboulaye. The response to the proposed statue was good, but they decided to wait until popular opinion on both sides of the Atlantic would be more widely sympathetic before mounting a public campaign. Bartholdi did, however, already begin developing his concept through sketches and a model.

The Statue of Liberty was intended to be a personification of Libertas, a Roman goddess of freedom who already adorned American coins and was popularly used in various artistic works at the time. She is depicted in neoclassical style, wearing a stola and pella, and on her head a diadem with seven rays forming a halo to represent the sun, the seven seas, and the seven continents. She holds a torch aloft to bring enlightenment to the world and stands over a broken chain. In her left hand, she holds a keystone-shaped tablet meant to represent the law upon which the date of Declaration of Independence is inscribed. In collaboration with engineer Gustave Eiffel, , the statue was made - standing just over 151 feet (46 m), and is a hollow figure made of thinly pounded copper sheets hammered over a steel framework. She was given as a gift from France during the centenary of American independence in 1876, and was in fact the result of cooperation between these two countries – France financing the statue, while the Americans would pay for the pedestal. It was hailed as one of the greatest technical achievements of the 19th century. Her formal name is "Liberty Enlightening the World." In 1984, it was designated as a UNESCO World Heritage Site

Definitely a must-see for all who aim to visit New York City – not only for the wonder that she inspires, but also for all the ideals she represents.

2. *Castle Clinton*

Originally known as West Battery or Southwest Battery, and subsequently named Castle Garden, Castle Clinton, or Fort Clinton, the fort is a circular sandstone construction located in Battery Park in Manhattan. It was the very first immigration station in America, and from 1855 to 1890, welcomed some 8 to 12 million people.

Originally built in 1811 on a small artificial island just offshore of the settlement of New Amsterdam, it was intended to be part of the fort system known as Castle Williams that was built to protect New York City from British naval attacks in the years leading up to the War of 1812. It was later named Fort Clinton in 1815 for the then-New York City Mayor DeWitt Clinton.

It was never used during that war. When Battery Park was later expanded using landfills, the fort became incorporated with the mainland of Manhattan. It served several other purposes including an entertainment center and restaurant, an exhibition hall and theater, and was more popularly known as Castle Garden. This is where the "Swedish Nightingale" Jenny Lind made her American debut.

From 1855 to 1890, it served as a sort of Emigrant Landing Depot, the nation's first ever immigrant processing facility. It is estimated that 2 out of 3 immigrants to the United States passed through the Castle Garden during this time. This was closed in 1890, and the operations were later on transferred to the much larger Ellis Island.

In 1941, it was the site of the New York City Aquarium. Throughout the years, it had been roofed over and extensively altered, although the original masonry of the fort was still retained. It was almost demolished in 1941 to make way for a crossing from Battery to Brooklyn, but was saved due to the efforts of preservationists. It was restored to its original design, and today is considered a national monument, and serves as a departure point for those wishing to visit Ellis Island or the Statue of Liberty. It now welcomes over 3 million visitors each year.

3. *Theodore Roosevelt Birthplace*

Theodore Roosevelt, Jr., 26th President of the United States, the driving force behind the Progressive Era and the Square Deal in the early 20th century, statesman, author, explorer, soldier, reformer, naturalist, and widely considered to be one of the greatest U.S. presidents – was born and raised for the first part of his life in Manhattan's 28 East 20th Street, New York City. Theodore Roosevelt was born there on October 27, 1858, and he and his family lived there until 1872, when they moved uptown to West 57th Street.

The three-story brownstone building as it now stands is not the original construction, however. That was demolished in 1916, until it was purchased by the Women's Roosevelt Memorial Association, now the Theodore Roosevelt Association, in 1919. The building was restored and recreated to a replica of what it originally was in 1865, and the row house next door was incorporated as a museum. Many of its furnishings were provided by the President's widow, Edith Carow, and his two sisters, Anna and Corinne, all of whom also supplied information for the recreation of the building.

The National Parks Service now offers tours of the site, and a visit can be most illuminating as to Theodore Roosevelt's childhood, his sickly condition, his desire to improve his physical constitution through exercise, and his great interest early on in being a naturalist. All of it becomes all the more illuminating when you consider his public persona as a Cowboy and Rough Rider Chief Executive whose face now stands alongside other luminaries as George Washington, Thomas Jefferson, and Abraham Lincoln on Mount Rushmore.

4. *African Burial Ground*

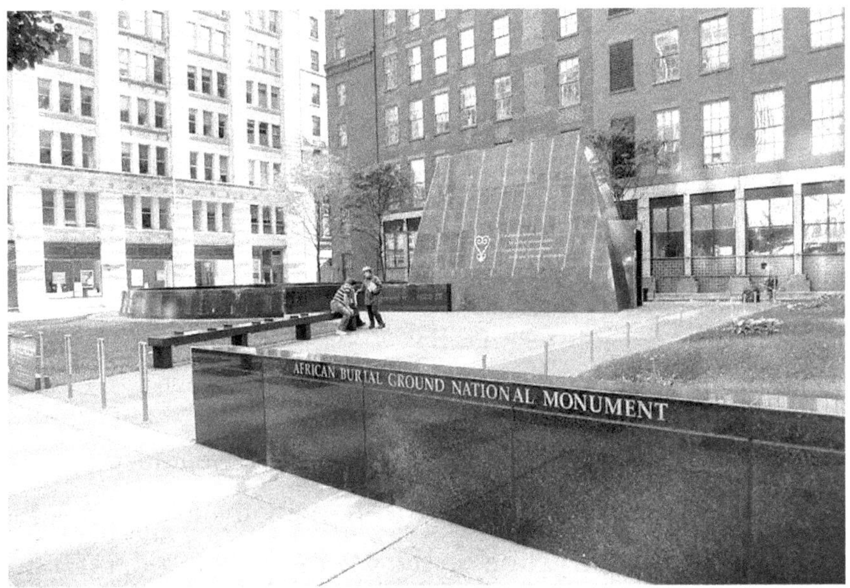

The African Burial Ground that is situated at Elk Street in Lower Manhattan is a National Monument that depicts one of the darker sides of New York City's history.

The discovery was made by General Services Administration (GSA) in October of 1991, during an archaeological survey and excavation for the construction of a new federal office building at 290 Broadway. Graves were discovered some 24 feet below ground, and hundreds of other bodies of what were determined to be black New Yorkers were also subsequently discovered in the area. Old maps had labeled this site as the "Negro's Burial Ground" – used around 1712 for the burial of enslaved and freed people of African descent. This was at the outskirts of what used to be the developed city, and mainly used because of a prohibition against the burial of those of African descent within the limits of the public cemetery of Trinity Church. It was estimated to have been used until 1794, until landfill was used to raise the grade of the land by some 25 feet in the late 1790s, and later on subdivided for the development of building lots. The country's first department store, A.T. Stewart Company Store, was erected on this lot, and the burial ground was largely forgotten.

After much controversy where some intact graves were found to have been broken up by the excavation, the proposed construction on the site of the new federal office building was redesigned to preserve part of the archeological site – for which a memorial was erected. It was listed in the National Register of Historic Places in 1992, and designated a National Historic Landmark in 1993. All in all, more than 400 intact remains of men, women and children were found, though it is estimated that some 15,000 to 20,000 Africans were buried here –the extent of the burial ground was too large to be fully excavated – it was the largest colonial-era cemetery for enslaved African people.

The memorial now features a granite monument with a map of the Atlantic area with reference to the "Circle of Diaspora" and the Middle Passage by which slaves were transported from Africa to North America. There is a "Door of No Return" which is intended to symbolize the slave ports on the coast of West Africa where many were sold by their native chiefs, never to see or return to their homeland again.

During the dedication of this memorial in 2007, Elk Street was officially renamed as the African Burial Ground Way. At the Ted Weiss Federal Building at 290 Broadway, there is also a visitor center which includes exhibits and displays regarding the lives of Africans in the early years of the country's and New York City's history.

5. *Green-Wood Cemetery and Battle Hill*

The first major battle of the American Revolutionary War took place on August 27, 1776, and is commonly known as The Battle of Long Island, the Battle of Brooklyn, or the

Battle of Brooklyn Heights. It is still considered the largest battle during the entire war, and Battle Hill the site of especially brutal fighting. Battle Hill is the highest point of what was then King's County, and is now located within Greenwood Cemetery.

The British Army were victorious during this battle, and they gained control of the strategically important city of New York and its harbor. Washington retreated to Manhattan, and after several more defeats, he and his army were driven out of New York entirely. There are several monuments to commemorate this difficult and bloody battle within the Cemetery itself, including:

- the Altar to Liberty, which includes a bronze statue of Minerva, located at the highest point of Brooklyn
- The Prison Ship Martyr's Monument as a memorial to all who died as prisoners on the British ships
- The Soldier's Monument, commemorating to 200 ill prisoners who were dumped on the beach of Milford
- The Old Stone House, a reconstructed farmhouse that was at the center of delaying tactics of the Marylanders

- Prospect Park along Battle Pass, which features a large granite boulder with a brass plaque and a marker for the Dongan Oak, which was felled to block the British advance.

It must be added, however, that Green-Wood Cemetery is not just a commemoration of the Battle of Long Island – it is also a commemoration of the lives that have been buried within its grounds in the years since then. Within cemetery grounds are wonderful, graphic monuments, tombstones and mausoleums of specific individuals, some famous, and some infamous – and tombs even of pets - whose lives are especially commemorated in a poignant way through the unique structures erected within these park-like grounds. The gently rolling hills of the terrain, and winding paths that twists and turns – where a person can literally get lost without a map – promises "a surprise around every bend."

6. *Grand Central Terminal*

Make a good start on your forays into the rest of New York City by starting with the terminus and origin of all New York City subway trains – the Grand Central Terminal. Even if you aren't planning on taking the subway to some other place that's interesting, you can probably spend a fascinating afternoon just exploring and discovering the nooks and crannies of this 100-year old depot.

Sometimes also referred to as Grand Central Station, or simply Grand Central, this rapid transit railroad terminal is located at 42nd Street and Park Avenue in Midtown Manhattan. The site's history as a transport terminal is long – and the current construction was essentially preceded by three different buildings intended to serve the same functions: The Grand Central Depot in 1871 which served railroad trains, the Grand Central Station in 1899-1900 serving steam trains, and the redesigned Grand Central Terminal which opened in 1913, servicing underground electric trains. To this day, it is the biggest terminal in the world, not only in the size of the building, but also in the number of tracks. In the years that followed, this monument was almost destroyed by the proposed construction of a tower intended to halt the financial decline of its then-owner, Penn Central Railroad. Prior to construction, however, Grand Central was declared a city landmark by the New York City Landmarks Preservation Commission. For the first time, the Supreme Court ruled on a case of historic preservation, upholding government land-use regulatory powers. Penn Central eventually went bankrupt.

The station continued its decline in the years that followed, with considerable destruction wrought by a bomb that exploded in 1876. It was only during the period of 1994-2000 that Grand Central underwent a massive overhaul, restoration and renovation under the auspices of the Metropolitan Transportation Authority who had signed a 280-year lease. The work was completed by 2007, and the terminal's centennial was celebrated on February 1, 2013.

The Grand Central Terminal today serves some 200,000 commuters, and in 2013, received some 21.6 million visitors. The building features magnificent Beaux-Arts architecture, with a cavernous Main Concourse with an elaborately decorated ceiling, a Dining Concourse below with seating and lounge areas and a fine selection of restaurants – including the oldest of them all, the Oyster Bar. Other points of interest in the station include Vanderbilt Hall, the elegant cocktail lounge at Campbell Apartment, the Whispering Gallery, the gourmet culinary market, and the "secret" elevated passageways for a magnificent view of the concourse. Whether you prefer to just walk around, or to take a tour, there is much to see in this famous New York City landmark.

7. *Ellis Island Immigration Museum*

The Ellis Island National Museum of Immigration is located in the Main Building on Ellis Island – the former immigration station complex. Located in Upper New York Bay, Ellis Island is originally a part of what used to be known as the Oyster Islands – three islands that were not completely submerged during high tide (the other two are Liberty Island and Black Tom Island). There was a rich source of oyster banks on these islands which have been a major food source since the original Lenape population until the next three centuries – until landfilling obliterated them. The island itself was named for Samuel Ellis, who acquired the island sometime in the late 1700's.

The original island itself was much smaller until it was expanded with land reclamation. For a time, it also served as a federal arsenal of the War Department, a military post and the location of Fort Gibson, until eventually being turned to a federal immigration station.

It is estimated that some 12 million immigrants entered America through the doors of Ellis Island. The Main Building as we know it today was constructed only after a fire of unknown origin destroyed the original wooden structures on the island – including all the immigration records dating back to 1855. The Main Building was designed in the French Renaissance Revival Style by Edward Lippincott Tilton and William A. Boring, who also designed the Kitchen and Laundry Building, the Main Powerhouse, and the Main Hospital Building. Due to the flood of immigrants, the island was subsequently expanded again with landfill, and additional structures built to accommodate the population.

After 1924, Ellis Island was used as a detention and deportation station for German merchant mariners and enemy aliens – mostly Axis nationals. It also served as a processing center for sick or wounded soldiers who were sent home, and as a Coast Guard training base. Immigration processing continued, though the numbers only picked up again after the war.

The Immigration station closed in November 1954, and the buildings fell into disrepair until it was restored and reopened in 1990. In 2015, it was officially renamed the Ellis Island National Museum of Immigration, and features exhibits which tell the story of American immigration, including the Hearing Room, Peak Immigration Years, the Peopling of America, Restoring a Landmark, Silent Voices, Treasures from Home, and the Ellis Island Chronicles. Audio tours are available, and the structures also include three theaters for films and live performances.

Outside, there is a Wall of Honor which contains a partial list of the immigrants who were processed on the island. It is estimated that some half of America's current population can trace their ancestry back to the immigrants who entered America through the doors of Ellis Island. A visit to this museum can be for many not just a historical New York trip, but also a familial one.

8. Brooklyn Bridge

Spanning more than 125 years, the hybrid cable-stayed/suspension bridge known as Brooklyn Bridge is an iconic part of the New York City landscape, and is also an amazing engineering feat of the 19th century as the first steel-wire suspension bridge ever constructed.

Crossing the East River to connect the boroughs of Manhattan and Brooklyn, the Brooklyn Bridge was designed by German immigrant and bridge and road builder John Augustus Roebling (who incidentally died during its construction), who dreamed of an alternative to ferry crossing across the East River. Interestingly, Brooklyn citizens decided in a close vote to become a borough of New York City some fifteen years after the opening of the Brooklyn Bridge, or in 1898.

To this day, Brooklyn Bridge has proven remarkably strong. There are two neo-Gothic style masonry towers to which numerous steel cables are attached, and for a time were the tallest structures in New York at 276 ft (84 m). The bridge spans a length of 5,989 ft, or about 1.8 km, across the East River, and has since provided ample passage for millions of commuters, tourists, trains, bicycles, pushcarts, and cars. An elevated pedestrian path provides people a chance to cross the river on foot across this monumental bridge without having to be bothered by the vehicular traffic below. This also offers pedestrians a wonderful view of the bridge towers and the Manhattan skyline.

Originally called the New York and Brooklyn Bridge and sometimes the East River Bridge, the Brooklyn Bridge was designated a National Historic Landmark in 1946 – just as its designer Roebling had predicted. It was renovated again from 2011 to 2015, in an effort to ensure the continued safety of those who crossed it.

9. The New York Public Library

The New York Public Library is actually a public library system consisting of different branches spread out in the boroughs of Manhattan, Staten Island, and The Bronx. It is considered the second largest public library in the United States, second only to the Library of Congress. It is also the fourth largest public library in the world – with a collection of some 53,000,000 books and other items. Its flagship building, also known as the Main Branch or simply the New York City Public Library, is the Schwartzman Building that is located on Fifth Avenue at 42nd Street in Midtown Manhattan.

The vast collection of the New York Public Library system was a combination of grass-roots libraries and the social libraries of the wealthy – including the Tilden bequest and the Carnegie donation. With generous funding from wealthy philanthropists, an imposing main branch was designed and constructed by Carerre and Hastings. The vision was for a huge reading room atop seven floors of bookstacks as the fastest system of getting books into the hands of those wanting to read them. The cornerstone of the building was laid down in May 1902, and the Main Building of the New York Public Library was officially opened on May of 1911 – after extensive interior work that resulted in some 75 miles of shelves.

The building itself is remarkable – the largest marble structure of thee time in the United States. It is marble and brick all the way through – some three feet of marble and an exterior constructed from 20,000 blocks of stone. It covers an area of 646,680 square feet and stretches a length of some 390 feet along Fifth Avenue.

The Main Building is considered as the apex of Beaux-Art design. There are two marble stone lions guarding the entrance – at one time having been called "Lord Astor" and "Lady Lenox" for the library founders, they were subsequently renamed "Patience" and "Fortitude" by Mayor La Guardia. There are flagpoles before the end pavilions with sculpted bronze bases with amazing detail and design. The interior is just as impressive – with an extensive mural in the Bill Blass Public Catalog Room and the famous Rose Main Reading Room. In 2008, the Main Building of the New York Public Library was renamed the Scharzman Building I honor of Stephen A. Scharzman, who donated $100 million for the renovation and expansion of the building – whose structure and elements had already begun to erode over time.

Another interesting side trip to a visit to the New York Public Library is the Library Way – a series of plaques depicting selected quotes from famous authors, poets, and other important personages. There are some 96 total plaques in all embedded along the north and south sides of 41st Street.

10. St Patrick's Cathedral

Built to accommodate the City's growing Catholic population, St. Patrick's Cathedral came after St. Peter's in the Financial District, and St. Patrick's Old Cathedral on Mulberry Street. It was designed by James Renwich, Jr., and named for the patron saint of Ireland.

Built along the Gothic Revival style, St. Patrick's has become a prominent landmark in New York City. It is still an active parish church, and is the seat of the archbishop of the Roman Catholic Archdiocese of New York. It spans an area the length of an entire city block, and while it certainly dominated the surroundings when it was first constructed in 1878, it still manages to hold its own even amidst the surrounding buildings and skyscrapers.

In 2012, St. Patrick's Cathedral underwent an extensive restoration that lasted for 3 years and cost some $177 million, and its original beauty once more shone after being the cleaning and repairs.

There is much to see. The building itself is made entirely of brick clad in marble. It has two prominent spires that rise to 330 feet (100.6 m) above street level. There are some 3,700 stained glass panels in the cathedral, including those in the Rose Window that rises above the entrance. Amazingly, the 9,000 pound bronze doors were designed so as to be easily opened even with one hand. It has a reproduction of Michelangelo's Pieta sculpted by William

Ordway Partridge, which is three times larger than Michelangelo's original. The cathedral's Stations of the Cross won an 1893 artistry prize at Chicago's World Columbian Exposition, and its Gallery Organ has one of the nation's most glorious wood facades.

You can join a guided tour to explore St. Patrick's Cathedral, or you can simply walk around to appreciate its exterior and interior details. Three to eight masses are held daily, and the cathedral is open daily from 6:30 a.m. to 8:45 p.m.

Chapter Six: Out And About In New York City

Exploration, some say, is best done by walking. You might not be able to walk to all the tourist spots below – a subway or bridge crossing is definitely called for in some – but once you do get to your chosen spot, your feet are your best friends.

Walking around and just looking, observing, paying attention, and appreciating can be one of the best ways to travel. See the sights, appreciate the unique architecture or simply bask in nature among the many wonderful parks in the city. You can climb up the tallest skyscrapers to get to the top, but once you're there, stop and just look around. The sights of New York City, Manhattan's iconic skyline, and the beautiful parks and charming architecture, all add to what make the City what it is.

1. Times Square

Times Square in Midtown Manhattan is known to many people the world over – recognizable for its colorful billboards and advertisements, and the lively packs of people joined together in the yearly celebration of New Year's Eve. It stretches from West 42nd to West 47th Streets, at the junction of Broadway and Seventh Avenue, and goes by many nicknames: The Crossroads of the World, The Center of the Universe, the Heart of the World, The Great White Way, and more commonly, the World's Busiest Intersection.

It is a center of the entertainment industry, both as a hub of Broadway Theaters as well as having been featured and highlighted many times in popular culture as quintessentially "New York."

It also has a long history. One might not easily consider this as a historical NYC site, but the truth is, there is perhaps no locale within New York City that has retained its importance as an epicenter of life, trade and culture as Times Square.

Its history dates back to the Dutch settlements, where it was called the "Great Kill" for three streams rich in fish and waterfowl. Subsequently, the Great Kill was known as a center of carriage-making, whereby it was named Longacre Square for London's Long Acre. The carriage industry grew, and lots were parceled off for hotels and other real estate construction as the population grew. It was called Times Square only in 1904 after the New York Times moved its headquarters to the Times Building. By this time, it was known as a low entertainment district with a theater, restaurants and cafes, and it was ablaze with electric lights and filled with throngs of people.

The first electrified advertisement appeared on the side of a bank in 1904, and Times Square was made the Eastern Terminus of the Lincoln Highway – the first road that ran across the United States, across 13 states from the western end in San Francisco, California. It grew as a cultural hub, however, only after World War II. The atmosphere generally degenerated, however, during the Great Depression and well into the 60's until the 1980's. By then it was considered a seedy neighborhood, dark and dangerous, filled with sex shops, adult theaters, and crime. The annual ball drop from the Times Square roof, however, which began since 1907, still continued.

The turnaround began from the 80's- 90's. A long-term development plan began to be implemented. The State of New York took possession of six historic theatres which subsequently underwent restoration and renovation. The area was cleaned up, undesirable elements were forced out, and more wholesome establishments set up. Today, it has evolved into a cultural epicenter with world-famous attractions including theater, amazing architecture, fine restaurants, and grand signage and billboards. It is still the center of the NYC New Year's Eve celebration where some 1-2 million people attend, and now accommodates around 330 pedestrians daily, and some 50 million visitors annually. It's a great thing to remember, too, that the last largest gathering in Times Square took place in August, 1945, when people celebrated the end of the Second World War.

2. *Central Park*

Central Park was not included in the original Commissioner's Plan of 1811, which set out the grid design for the streets of Manhattan. The need for a great public part was strongly felt by many, however – especially with New York City's population nearly quadrupling rom 1821-1855. As a result, 700 acres (280 ha) of land from 59th to 106th Streets were designated for the creation of the park – the land alone costing more than $5M. A landscape design was held by the Central Park Commission in 1857, and the "Greensward Plan" by Frederick Law Olmsted and Calvert Vaux was selected. Construction took place from between 1860 to 1873.

Several renovations of Central Park took place throughout the years – interspersed with years of neglect, decline, and failed maintenance. With each renovation, however, there was a desire to adhere to the original purpose of an idyllic landscape for a park that was also used for recreational purposes.

There are numerous points of interest within the park itself – some landscaped vistas of beautiful surroundings, others geared towards recreational activities. Some of its more notable features include the Harlem Meer, The Reservoir, The Great Lawn, The Lake, and the Pond. There are extensive walking tracks, bridle paths, two ice-skating rinks, a zoo, a conservatory garden, wildlife sanctuary, and an outdoor amphitheater. There are enclosed playgrounds for children, some seven major lawns, and indoor attractions such as the Belvedere Castle and the Swedish Cottage Marionette Theatre. There is a Visitors' Center at the Dairy that leads to Bethesda Terraces, a Strawberry Garden, and Shakespeare's Garden. There are at least 29 sculptures within the park; it is home to a rich diversity of flora and fauna, contains at least two indoor restaurants, and myriad other attractions for hobbyists or those simply looking for a place to sit down and enjoy nature.

As always, however, the original intent was preserved – that of naturalistic landscapes designed with separate circulation systems for various traffic such as pedestrians, horseback riders, and pleasure vehicles.

A trip to New York should definitely include a visit to Central Park. It isn't likely that you will be able to cover the entire grounds in one day, much less one afternoon – though why would you? Central Park is a place to enjoy nature, to partake of the "lungs of New York," to sit a spell and just relax, or to challenge yourself in one outdoor or sports activity or another. You can bet that this most visited park in the United States will still have some surprises for you the next time you visit. As parks go, it's not one you would ever consider boring, predictable, or even dull. And best of all, it's completely free.

3. *Empire State Building*

For nearly 40 years, the Empire State Building stood as the world's tallest building – from its construction in 1931 until it was topped by the North Tower of the original World Trade Center in 1970. It was subsequently also "overshadowed" by the One World Trade Center that saw construction in 2012. Today, it ranks as the 2th tallest skyscraper in the world – the fifth tallest in the United

States. It has a roof height of 1, 250 ft (381 m), and when its antenna spire is included, stands at a total of 1, 454 ft (443 m) high. It totals 102 stories, is the tallest structure leading in Energy and Environmental Design, and is undoubtedly one of the most recognizable architectural icons of New York City and the United States.

The building was designed by William Lamb from the firm Shreve, Lamb and Harmon, and construction began in 1930. It was part of a competition for the world's tallest building – the two other competitors being 40 Wall Street and the Chrysler Building. As the construction of the Empire State Building progressed, however, these two competitors were eventually eclipsed. Ironically, it was a mostly empty building for the first years after it opened – due to an inconvenient location to public transportation, and because of the onset of the Great Depression. At the time, people referred to it as the "Empty State Building."

The interior of the Empire State Building is now mostly commercial and office spaces – though most tourists flock to the indoor and outdoor observation deck on the 86th floor. The other 16 stories feature an art deco tower with a 203 ft (62 m) pinnacle. This is mostly covered with broadcast antennas, and at the very tip is a lightning rod. Nearly all the city's commercial broadcast stations transmit from the top of the Empire State Building. Its base covers an area of about 2 acres, has 73 elevators and houses 1,000 some 1,000 business at which approximately 21,000 employees work. Being the second largest single office complex in America (second only to the Pentagon), the Empire State Building has its own zip code.

There is an exhibit of the building's construction, as well as a gift shop, on the 80th floor. The Observation Deck on the 86th floor can be reached by elevators or stairs, and from this vantage point the visitor can have a wonderful 360-degree view of the city of New York. A much smaller, but enclosed Observation Deck is located on the 102nd floor. These have been visited by over 110 million people, and the queues to enter are record long – so if you are planning to visit the Observation Deck, be sure to book your tickets in advance, and arrive early so you don't end up spending so much of your time waiting in line.

There is also a complementary motion simulator ride located on the 2nd floor, too – this is a simulation of an aerial tour over the city. But perhaps the one other notable feature of the Empire State Building are its lights. The colors change by season, by holiday, by evens, and even in commemoration of the passing of certain celebrated personalities such as Frank Sinatra, Fay Wray, and the tragedy of the destruction of the World Trade Center. To be able to truly appreciate these light displays, however, one needs to be at a vantage point some distance from the building, and with a good view.

4. Washington Square Park

This public park located in Greenwich Village has a pretty interesting history preceding its current and rather bucolic setting. It was once referred to as "The Land of the Blacks" – land given to slaves by the Dutch who intended them to serve as a buffer against hostile Native Americans. It was mainly used as farmland, until 1797, when a portion of the land was purchased by the Common Council of New York to serve as a public burial ground, or a potter's field. And it certainly served as a convenient hygienic measure as the resting place of those who died from the yellow fever epidemic in the early 19th century – at the time, this area was outside the city limits. Later on, it was also the location of a public gallows an execution ground. To date, there is an estimated 20,000 bodies are still buried under Washington Square.

In 1826, additional land to the west was bought by the City, and the entire area was converted into the Washington Military Parade Ground. This was a public place where volunteer militia trained. To the north of the park, a row of Greek Revival Style houses were built from 1829 to 1833, which are now referred to as "The Row."

Washington Square Park features two prominent landmarks: the Washington Square Arch and the Washington Square Fountain that honor their namesake, George Washington, among other notable statues and monuments. Today, it is a very interactive park – and draws people from all walks of life, serving as a gathering place for avant-garde artists such as street performers, musicians, poets, chess enthusiasts, and a playground for children. It has also been a popular gathering place for rallies, protests and demonstrations ever since the commemorative march for the Triangle Shirtwaist Factory fire of 1912, where 146 workers were killed the year before. The outdoor chess tables are often referred to as the Manhattan's "chess district," and a number of chess shops have opened up in the surroundings to cater to this special crowd.

It's a great place to go to relax, enjoy nature, watch people, go for a walk among the paved paths, play chess, or to just sit back and relax at the numerous available benches.

5. *Chrysler Building*

If you're fond of skyscrapers and cars, then the Chrysler Building should definitely be on your list during your New York City trip. This is a 77-story building with a very distinctive shiny peak that has become almost iconic of the New York City skyline. And to top it all off, Walter Chrysler had Architect William Van Alen add decorative features that were inspired by Chrysler's automobile designs – including stainless steel eagle head hood ornaments, Chrysler radiator caps and even a notable shiny vertex.

For a very brief moment after its construction in 1930, or for eleven months, the Chrysler Building was the tallest building in the world – until it was eventually surpassed in height by the Empire State Building. Nevertheless, the Chrysler Building is still a magnificent example of Art Deco architecture, and a testament to the age of automobiles. It has since then become one of the most beloved and very popular structures in New York City – a literal jewel-like crown that lights up the city skyline at night.

Rather unfortunately, the public observation deck that used to exist at the top of the building is no longer open to the public – it closed in 1945, and people are only allowed until the lobby. That doesn't mean you can't appreciate the beauty and unique structure of the Chrysler Building – whether from ground level, or from a vantage point from a different building – particularly from the Visitors' Center and Observation Deck of the Empire State Building. Then, there is the trip into the lobby, which might not seem like much initially, but which might give you a unique Art Deco interior surprise – from the red Moroccan marble walls, the marble floors, the beautiful designs for the double bank elevators, and the extensive and amazing mural on the ceiling entitled "Transport and Human Endeavor" – a work of art by Edward Trumbull.

Being a functioning office building, it is good to remember that the Chrysler Building's lobby is only open to the public from 8 a.m. to 6 p.m. from Monday to Friday.

6. *Wall Street*

It has been said that Wall Street was named after the northern wall or boundary of "New Amsterdam" that was built to protect the Dutch from both the British and American Indian tribes in the area. This wall was subsequently strengthened due to increasing tensions with the creation of a double palisade – and the space between these two walls was like a street that eventually became called Wall Street.

Somewhat tragically, Wall Street was a central marketplace that was also the city's first official slave market – for the sale and rental of enslaved Africans and Indians. Later on, traders and speculators gathered and traded securities at a buttonwood tree that stood at the foot of Wall Street. In 1792, they formalized their association through the Buttonwood Agreement, which is the origin of today's New York Stock Exchange. To this day, it is the recognized center of the financial market of the United States, and the heart of New York City's Financial District.

Wall Street for 0.7 mile from Broadway to South Street in the Financial District of Lower Manhattan, and is home to two of the world's largest stock exchanges according to total market capitalization: the New York Stock Exchange, and NASDAQ.

This is an old district – where streets were laid out prior to the Commissioner's Plan of 1811. There are still streets that are barely wide enough to accommodate a single lane of traffic. It is also home to some breathtaking architecture, however, that is rooted in the Gilded Age. Some of the notable buildings include Federal Hall, Bankers Trust Company Building, The Trump Building, and the New

York Stock Exchange – the latter of which is a key anchor for the area.

Wall Street is also boasted by New York City as a major tourist destination, and tours highlight the history, the unique architecture, and attractions such as the gold vault beneath the Federal Reserve. There is a sense of the financial and economic power in Wall Street, though sometimes with the negative connotations of elitism, capitalism, and financial interests. Perhaps this is why Wall Street is so compelling as a tourist attraction – power and wealth and an association with some of the most wealthy names in New York City history.

A unique feature of Wall Street is the Charging Bull Statue, which represents a constantly rising market, i.e., a "bull market." This is located in front of the New York Stock Exchange until it was moved to Bowling Green – a small annex park near Wall Street. It is one of the area's most popular attractions, and many superstitiously rub him for good luck!

7. The High Line

The High Line, or High Line Park, is a linear park built on a disused elevated railway of the New York Central Railroad. This was the West Side Line that used to carry freight trains from 34th Street to St. John's Park Terminal at Spring Street. It was designed particularly to go through, instead of over, the avenue, and connections directly with factories and warehouses enabled easy loading and unloading of cargo within the buildings.

With the growth of interstate trucking, however, rail traffic diminished to the extent that the West Line was hardly in use. The last train that operated on the line was in 1980.

What ensued were arguments and debates in the 80s between those who wanted the structure demolished, and railroad enthusiasts who argued for preservation. A small section was demolished in 1991, and the structure lay mostly unused and in disrepair. Nature began to take over the lines, however, and during the 1990s, people noted the grass, shrubs, and certain hardy trees that sprang up amidst the gravel of the railway line. By this time, plans for the lines demolition were also being looked into.

In 1999, a nonprofit organization called Friends of the High Line, who were mostly residents of the neighborhood through which the line ran through, was formed. They advocated for the preservation of the high line and its repurposing as a public open space or an elevated park or greenway. They looked to the Promenade Plantee in Paris for inspiration. Photographs of the now half-wild high line were used as a reference in the ensuing discussions, and public support for the proposed redevelopment grew. Funding was sought, and in 2006, construction began.

The Park was opened successively opened to the public in three phases, dependent on the progress of construction, and with it came the revitalization of Chelsea. This also provided a growth in the nearby real estate development, and inspired other neighborhoods to try unique ways of gentrifying their own districts.

Today, the High Line draws a growing number of tourists, and the Friends of the High Line have begun offering tours and cultural events that take place on the High Line, such as art and garden exhibits, and seasonal shows and performances.

8. *Bryant Park*

The New York Public Library is located just at the eastern boundary of Bryant Park, and one interesting fact about this proximity is that the park is located entirely over an underground structure where the library's stacks are stored.

Originally a potter's field or graveyard for the poor, it was converted to a park after the bodies buried beneath were moved to Wards Island. The first park that stood on this same site was known as Reservoir Square in 1847 but later renamed Bryant Park in honor of abolitionist and New York Evening Post editor William Cullen Bryant, in 1884. Construction of the Main Building of the New York Public Library began afterwards, in 1899.

It has been called the "Town Square of Midtown" by a 1995 New York Times article – most of the people who frequent Bryant Park are office workers, city visitors, and revelers. In order to encourage this type of public presence, various amenities catering to the white collar professionals. Features include a custom-built carousel, clean restrooms, an open-air library, and food and drinks served at several kiosks, grills and cafés. It is also the first park in New York to have provided free WiFi access to visitors.

Some of the more notable features of the Park include the Great Lawn where a rally for the Moratorium to end the War in Vietnam took place in 1969. Various sculptures dot the park, and best of all, a Winter Village around the free-admission skating rink that certainly draws a crowd during the holidays.

A quiet, relaxing and comfortable park to visit – complete with amenities, and hailed by the New York City Parks Commissioner Benepe as "the gold standard for park comfort stations."

9. Staten Island Ferry

Want some of the best and breathtaking views of the Manhattan skyline, the Statue of Liberty, and the New York Harbor, for free? Try a ride on the Staten Island Ferry – it isn't just a means of transportation. It's also a 25-minute overland moving view deck for some of the most stunning sighs of New York City. And did we mention that it's free?

Ferry services are available 24 hours a day, every day – usually around every 30 minutes. Ferries depart Manhattan from the Staten Island Ferry Whitehall Terminal at the South Ferry, near Battery Park, and arrives and then departs from the St. George Terminal on Richmond Terrace in Staten Island. It is estimated that the ferries carry over 21 million passengers annually.

The Staten Island Ferry is perhaps the only remaining vestige of what was once the extensive ferry system of New York City.

10.Brooklyn Botanic Garden

The Brooklyn Botanic Garden is located in the borough of Brooklyn within the Prospect Park neighborhood.

Founded in 1910, the garden was initially called Institute Park, before its name was subsequently changed to Brooklyn Botanic Garden in 1911.

The garden covers a wide area of about 52 acres, and was designed by landscape architect Harold Caparn, and features specialty gardens and collections within the Garden. A stroll through the BBG can therefore yield a wide variety of beautiful landscapes – all located within a single park.

Some of the specialty gardens include the Cherry Trees, The Japanese Hill-and-Pond Garden, Native Flora Garden, the Shakespeare Garden, The Cranford Rose Garden, The Children's Garden, and The Alice Recknagel Ireys Fragrance Garden. Structures within the Garden include the Steinhardt Conservatory and the C.V. Starr Bonsai Museum, climate themed plant pavilions, and a white-cast iron and glass aquatic plant house. There is also an art gallery and a Visitor Center and Gardener's Resource Center.

The Brooklyn Botanic Garden supports research and education, as well as community horticultural programs – offering classes on various topics, and resources for Urban Composting Projects.

A worthwhile, breathtaking, and enlightening place to visit. You should definitely check it out during a visit to New York.

Chapter Seven: Interacting With New York

There are plenty of activities and things to do in New York that can enliven and enrich a visit to the City. From immersing yourself in the different cultural features of New York City's ethnic communities, to watching the next big game, visiting the iconic Coney Island, or taking part in one of many of New York City's musical events, interacting with New York means joining the local residents in some of the events that help define New York City life and culture.

1. *Film Forum*

What better way to truly appreciate New York's reputation for being a cinematic epicenter than by attending one of its iconic nonprofit theater gems. Located at 209 West Houston Street in Hudson Square, Manhattan, Film Forum began in 1970 as an alternative screening space for indie films. Today, it has grown to a 3-screen cinema with nearly 500 seats. It is open 365 days a year, and offers the public a variety of indie films, foreign art films, American classics, and other somewhat high-brow theatrical releases. The films are always well-selected, and the community are generally in sync in their appreciation of fine movies.

This may not be the right place to bring along kids, but the small and intimate theatres are a great place for film buffs to settle down and enjoy some amazing, rare, or just simply new and refreshing footage.

2. Chinatown

Part of what characterizes New York culture is the confluence of different cultures that have made New York City what it is today. With a long history rooted in immigration, it is only to be expected that various cultures would seek to put down their roots in their new home, keeping as much of their culture alive as possible. A trip through New York can literally bring you all over the world and through different continents. And one of the densest immigrant populations in New York today are the Chinese – who are mostly centered in Chinatown.

There are some nine Chinatown neighborhoods scattered throughout New York City, and as many as twelve in the New York metropolitan area. The ethnic Chinese population in New York is the largest outside of Asia, and

Chinatown in Lower Manhattan is considered to be the oldest of the Chinese ethnic enclaves.

The first of the Chinese immigrants in New York City was Ah Ken, a Cantonese businessman, who arrived in the area in the 1840s. By 1882, there were some 2,000 Chinese immigrants, and more than 7,000 in 1900. But because of the Chinese Exclusion Act of 1943, most of the residents were men, and tongs (whether legitimate associations or crime syndicates or gangs) dominated the life in Chinatown, which grew around Ah Ken's smoke shop on Park Row.

After the enactment of the Immigration and Nationality Act of 1965, more Asian immigrants poured into the country, and Chinatown grew. Around the 80s and 90s, the population grew so much that many began migrating elsewhere – foremost of which to Brooklyn. Rising rent prices in Manhattan also had immigrant Chinese seeking their homes elsewhere in the City, such as in Elmhurst and Flushing in Queens and East Harlem in Upper Manhattan. Meanwhile, Chinatown in Manhattan continued to grow and thrive.

There are plenty of things to do and see on a visit to Chinatown. There are lots of places to shop, plenty of eateries ,wholesalers, and places where you can buy herbal remedies! It can also be an exploration of the Chinese immigrant history and culture, when you visit notable spots such as the Mahayana Buddhist Temple and the Museum of Chinese in America. Admire distinctive sculptures in the area such as the Kimlau Memorial Arch, the statue of Lin Ze Xu, and the Confucius Statue.

Immerse yourself in the local culture by visiting Columbus Park – if you get there early in the morning, you can ask to join the group practicing tai-chi. Or simply indulge in the color, sights, sounds, and smells of Chinatown.

3. *Coney Island*

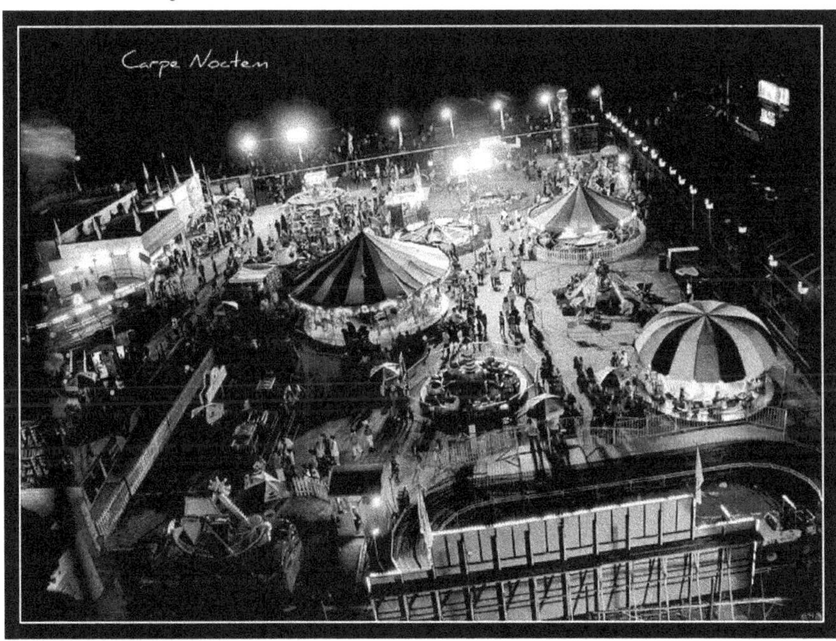

Looking for something a bit more afield than the Manhattan culture of New York? Why not travel a bit more afield to the peninsula of Coney Island with its amusement parks and seaside resorts??

Lying on a peninsula in the southwestern borough of Brooklyn, some of the first amusement and entertainment structures were built on Coney Island in the 1840s. In 1829, after the construction of Coney Island Hotel, this peninsula started to grow into a popular resort area. It was near enough, and yet some distance from, both Brooklyn and Manhattan that it wasn't difficult to conceive of a stay at Coney Island as a vacation. More hotels and resorts were built, businesses were established in the area, and the tourists began to arrive.

There are at least two amusement parks remaining on Coney Island – Luna Park and Deno's Wonder Wheel Amusement Park – with several other attractions and events. Three of these rides have, in fact, been listed in the National Register of Historic Places: the Wonder Wheel which dates back to 1918-1920, the Cyclone dating back to 1927 and one of the world's oldest wooden rollercoasters, and the Parachute Jump from the 1939 New York World's Fair. Of course, there are other rides and attractions such as the Thunderbolt, the B&B Carousel, Bumper Cars, and Haunted Houses.

On the other hand, the beaches of Coney Island are open to all without restrictions, and are served more than adequately by the Riegelmann Boardwalk. There are plenty of places to eat on Coney Island – served by the various ethnicities that make up its population. The richness and diversity of the place only serve to add to neighborhood's appeal and charm.

4. *Yankee Stadium*

There is certainly something for everyone in New York City, and that goes for sports fans, too. Located in the Bronx, the Yankee Stadium is the home ballpark of the New York Yankees of Major League Baseball. It is also the home stadium of the New York City FC in Major League Soccer.

The New York Yankee Stadium which draws so many crowds now is actually not the same in which Babe Ruth and the New York Yankees prime years. The 8 acre original lies one block to the south – given over now to a public park called Heritage Field. The new Yankee Stadium was constructed over what used to be the 24 acre Macombs Dam Park. Overall, it is considered to be the most expensive stadium ever built.

Utilizing many of the elements of the original Yankee stadium, the new stadium was opened in 2009 – and that same year, the New York Yankees won the 2009 World Series in the new stadium.

The stadium itself has a seating capacity of 4,300, with 68 luxury suites. There is a greater ballpark space, and increased amenities inside. The exterior of the stadium mirrored the original stadium as closely as possible – using Indiana limestone, granite, and pre-cast concrete, with the building's name in gold letters above each gate. Within, there walls are linked with hundreds of photographs of the playing history of the Yankees – derived from a cooperation with several news and media organizations. There is also a New York Yankees Museum located at the lower level of Gate 6, displaying a wide range of Yankees' memorabilia. There are a wide range of restaurants inside, with some of them offering installed TV monitors with reduced seat prices. It is a fully equipped stadium with many useful amenities for sports fans – and for those who can afford the somewhat pricey tickets – a magnificent experience to be able to watch a great game within a grand stadium.

5. *Bronx Zoo*

With an area of 265 acres (107 ha), the Bronx Zoo is the largest metropolitan zoo in the United States, and numbers among the largest zoo in the world.

The Bronx Zoo traces its roots to the Wildlife Conservation Society, initially called the New York Zoological Society, that was founded in 1895. They were composed mostly of members of the Boone and Crockett Club. The purpose of the organization was the founding of a zoo, the promotion of the study of zoology, and the preservation of wildlife.

The Bronx Zoological Park was opened to the public on November 8, 1899, with 22 exhibits featuring 843 animals. In 1916, the zoo built the word's first animal hospital. By 2010, the zoo was home to more than 4,000 animals of some 650 species – many of which are endangered or threatened.

The exhibits are myriad, and although the zoo allowed free admission on Wednesdays, tickets are required for the rest of the week. Tickets also vary between General Admission, which allow access to free exhibits, and premium exhibits that require additional fees. For a Total Experience plan, one has access to all the exhibits.

Some of the free exhibits include the African Plains, Baboon Reserve, Big bears, Madagascar!, Aquatic Bird House, Tiger Mountain, World of Reptiles, Birds of Prey, and Bison Range, among others. Premium tickets allow access to some attractions such as the Bug Carousel, the Butterfly Garden, Congo Gorilla Forest, Jungle World, and Zoo Shuttle. They also offer a Premium Family Membership which allows free unlimited admission to five other zoos: Bronx Zoo, Central Park Zoo, Prospect Park Zoo, Queens Zoo, and the New York Aquarium. This membership comes with an annual fee.

6. *Madison Square Garden*

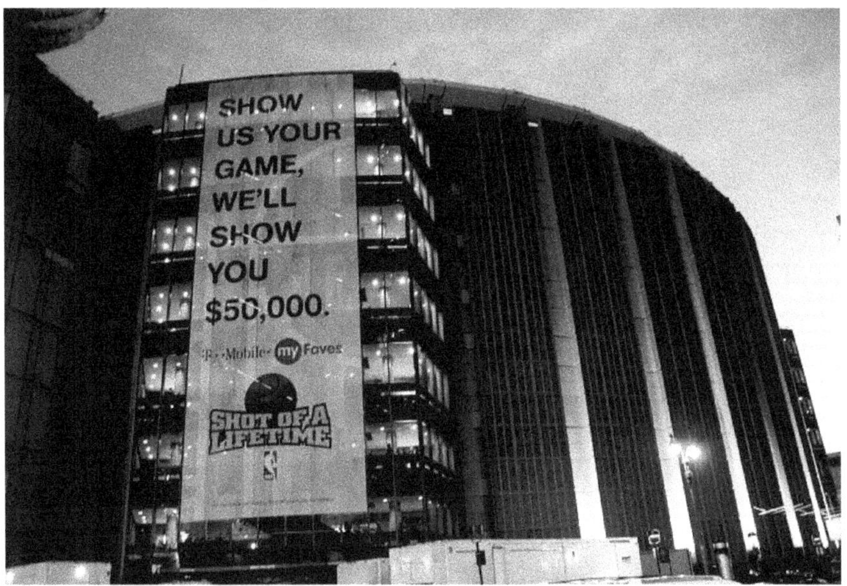

Ever wanted to watch a live professional basketball game? Ice hockey? Or maybe a live concert of your favorite artist? Within this celebrated arena, iconic athletes and chart-topping performers and musicians have made history under the watchful eyes of 19,500 seats of roaring fans. Whatever the event, you can't afford not to take part in the celebrations of artistry and sportsmanship that take place within The Garden.

Madison Square Garden was named after James Madison, the fourth President of the United States, and the one in use today is actually the fourth building to be called by this name. Today's arena opened to the public in 1986, though it has undergone several renovations since then.

Madison Square Garden regularly hosts sporting events, concerts, and various other significant events. Check out their upcoming schedules, and if you find an event you don't want to miss, go ahead and book a ticket. You can even join one of the guided tours that are given every day, and get a look behind the scenes.

7. *Barclays Center*

Much as it is with the Madison Square Garden, the Barclays Center in Booklyn also provides a good venue for sports, concerts and other significant events.

This unique design for a multipurpose indoor arena sits partially on a platform over the Long Island Rail Road at Atlantic Avenue. It is home to the Brooklyn Nets and the

New York Islanders of the National Hockey League. Barclay's certainly holds its own compared to other similar venues in the Metropolitan Area, even the famed Madison Square Garden.

The Barclay Center's architecture is characterized by three articulated bands featuring a glass curtain wall that is composed of preweathered steel panels in a kind of "latticework" that is designed to evoke Brooklyn's brownstones. There is a 117 by 56 foot oculus outside of the main entrance with an irregularly shaped display screen looping the interior face of the oculus. This allows people in the plaza to view the scoreboard in the arena's floor location.

The arena was named Barclays Center after the London-based banking group Barclays who was reported to have paid for naming rights.

Some of the notable events that take place inside this new arena include NBA basketball games, college basketball games, NHL Hockey, and various other sports matches such as boxing and wrestling events. It is also a very conducive venue for musical concerts – in 2013, they hosed the MTV Video Music Awards, the first time it took place in New York outside of Manhattan.

Being able to take part in any of the major events taking place inside Barclays Center is a wonderful way to immerse yourself in New York life and culture during your visit.

8. *Astoria*

Immerse yourself in one of the most culturally diverse neighborhoods in New York that caters to the middle class. In Astoria, Queens, you can experience a variety of international cuisines for a price range that won't break your budget.

Known primarily for its Greek traditional neighborhood, Astoria is also home to a number of other ethnic communities – Italian, Brazilian, Baltic, Irish, and Egyptians. Of late, younger, hip crowds have also begun to move in to the middle class neighborhood, infusing fresh life into this quiet spot in Queens.

This is a great place to food-trip your way around a variety of international cuisines. As many as five continents are represented among the different restaurants available in the area – and some would say they are far more authentic, and certainly not quite so expensive – as those served in the elegant restaurants in Manhattan.

And together with the food comes the culture, so shops and stores abound, selling a variety of interesting things – Greek groceries, vintage clothing, Eastern European meats, locally made accessories and clothing. There's no shortage of shopping opportunities while you're there.

And if that isn't enough, Astoria also offers one of the oldest of New York City beer gardens: Bohemian Hall & Beer Garden, which has been in operation since 1910. There are other beer gardens that have since sprung up in the City, so you won't be short on choices. For a more beer-centered experience, there are even a number of burgeoning local breweries and home-brew equipment stores.

And finally, take a moment to enjoy the outdoors of Astoria's neighborhood. Astoria Park is a leafy, 60 acre park set on gently sloping hills with a good view of the East River. There are playgrounds, running tracks, a skating park, and the City's oldest and largest swimming pool. And to further bolster the neighborhood's unique diversity – there are a number of Green sculptures in Athens Square Park. There is plenty of music and dancing, too – whether you opt to join the locals in the Tuesday Greek Nights, or the Wednesday Italian Nights. A visit to Astoria can be a relaxing and enjoyable outing for the entire family.

9. *Madame Tussauds*

Madame Tussauds New York opened to the public in 2000, and is part of the "Madame Tussauds" museums owned by Merlin Entertainment. The Madame Tussauds wax museums originated from London, based on the works of Marie Tussaud, who opened her first museum in 1835. Since then, the Madame Tussauds Wax Museums have become a major tourist attraction throughout the world, with wax figures ranging from historical and royal figures to film stars, and famous musicians.

Madame Tussauds New York City is located on 42nd Street, close to Times Square, and contains 5 floors of over 200 figures on display, and certainly one of the most popular destinations in New York City today.

Some of the notable wax figures of Madame Tussauds include actors like Leonardo DiCaprio, Julia Roberts, Jennifer Aniston; musicians like Rihanna, Taylor Swift and Katy Perry, athletes Muhammad Ali and Lionel Messi, Iconic characters as Marilyn Monroe and Charlie Chaplin, fictional characters, and even political leaders.

One notable thing about Madame Tussauds New York is the absence of ropes or barriers around the wax figures, so getting a picture or a selfie with any one of the celebrities and eminent figures you admire is very possible. Sure they're made of wax, but they do seem amazingly life-like!

10. New York City Pizza

Want to immerse yourself more in New York City culture? Try a pizza!

Ask a New Yorker and they'll tell you that they are both passionate and serious about their pizza. So you simply can't not try what they consider the best pizzas in town while you're in the City!

Here's a rundown of some of the more popular pizza parlors in the City. Take your pick, and enjoy!

- John's of Bleecker Street on Bleecker Street
- Don Antonio by Starita on West 50th Street
- Motorino on 139 Broadway, Brooklyn
- Artichoke Basille's Pizza & Brewery on 328 E 14th Street

- Di Fara Pizza on 1424 Avenue J, Brooklyn
- Franny's at Flatbush Ave., Brooklyn
- Grimaldi's Pizza, Brooklyn
- Joe and Pat's Pizzeria on Staten Island
- Lee's Tavern at Hancock Street, Staten Island
- Lombardi's Coal Oven Pizza, the oldest one in town, is on Spring Street, New York
- Paulie Gee's at 60 Greenpoint Avenue, Brooklyn
- Speedy Romeo, at 376 Classon Avenue, Brooklyn
- Roberta's, 261 Moore Street, Brooklyn
- Best Pizza, 33 Havemeyer Street, Brooklyn
- Totonno's, 1524 Neptune Aveue, Brooklyn
- Louie & Ernie's Pizza , 1300 Crosby Avenue, Bronx

Chapter Eight: The New York City Night Scene

New York City is the "city that never sleeps." And there are certainly plenty of things for people to do or to go even after the sun goes down.

There's a certain vibrancy lent to the City when night falls and the distinctive city skyline is lit by thousands and millions of winking lights. And where there are people who don't sleep, there are places where they can go. New York City boasts some of the best live performances on amazing stages – whether dance, opera, or concerts. Want something a little less stuffy and a bit more free? New York City offers a great variety of diverse nightspots that you should definitely check out. Or if you're the more quiet type – joining any of the many tours by night can be a great and memorable experience, too.

Not sure where to start? Here's a few ideas to get you started!

1. *The Bowery Ballroom*

For some excellent acoustics, historical aura, and indie rock, the Bowery Ballroom is an excellent place to visit. Located in the Bowery section of Manhattan, the Bowery Ballroom is part of the Bowery Presents Organization that runs and promotes several music and concert venues – at least five others in New York City, as well as in Boston, Philadelphia, Atlanta, and Maine.

The original structure at 6 Delancey Street was a Beaux Arts construction intended to replace an earlier three-story brick theater. What remained of this theater was only the stone foundation, which is still recognizable in the lower-level lounge.

Soon after the construction of 6 Delancey, however, the stock market crashed in 1929. It was vacant throughout the Great depression and the Second World War, until it was eventually occupied by several business concerns which included a jewelry store, a haberdashery, and Treemark Shoes. Eventually, lighting and carpet stores utilized the space, until 1997, when the Bowery Ballroom took over and the space was converted into a music venue.

It was named Bowery Ballroom for the Bowery Songs album of Joan Baez, which was recorded at a live concert at the Bowery Ballroom in November 6, 2004. It currently seats some 550 people, and despite extensive renovations to support a state of the art sound system and equipment, much of the original construction remains – brass rails, brass and iron metalworks, mahogany-lined VIP rooms, and the coffer-vaulted plaster ceiling in the downstairs bar – all lending a unique atmosphere to a place that caters to music lovers with indie-rock leanings.

2. *Broadway Theatre*

New York City is a cultural epicenter as much as it is a central business and financial district, and at the heart of its world class entertainment is Broadway and the performing arts scene – generally considered to rival London's West End theatres in terms of English-speaking commercial theatre productions.

There are at least 41 professional theatres, many venues of which have a long and rich history, located along the Theater District of Midtown Manhattan, with dramas, plays, and musicals being shown every night of the week.

Broadway shows are one of the most popular tourist attractions in New York City today. In 2010, more than $1 billion in tickets, were sold; from 215-2016, total attendance was estimated to be at more than 13 million, with grosses at more than $1 billion. The longest running musical in Broadway history is The Phantom of the Opera, which opened in 1988 in Broadway, and is still going strong today.

Check out the currently running shows on Broadway, and book your tickets early if there's something you wish to see. Given the great variety of what are offered, chances are you'll find a good selection of performances you'll definitely be interested in. Treat yourself to a night of Broadway while you're visiting New York City.

3. *Apollo Theater*

The building which now houses Apollo Theater was designed in the neo-Classical style in 1914, and was originally intended to be a Burlesque Theater. Ironically, given the important role that the Apollo played in the African-American music growth, it had a "Whites-Only" policy when the burlesque theater first operated.

The theater fell into disrepair and eventually closed in the early 1930s, after which it was bought by Sidney Cohen.

It was lavishly renovated and thereafter opened as the Apollo Theater – a music hall that catered to the black community of Harlem. One of the first major stars to appear in the Apollo Theater was jazz singer and Broadway star Adelaide Hall.

Apollo Theater faced some tough competition at the time with other music venues such as Lafayette and the Harlem Opera House. When owner Cohen died, Apollo Theater and the Harlem Opera House merged. But while Harlem Opera House changed to a movie theater, Apollo Theater remained a stage where some of the best African American acts were shown.

One distinctive feature that Apollo had was amateur night, where amateurs to the music industry could have their time on stage. There was an "executioner" who swept performers off the stage if they displeased the audience, or they would be chased by a stagehand off the stage with a cap pistol and the sound of a siren.

Amateur Night became known as the place where stars are born and legends are made – and central to the Harlem Renaissance of the 1920s. Some of the world famous artists who made their debut at the Apollo Theater include Ella Fitzgerald, Thelma Carpenter, Jimi Hendrix, Billie Holiday, Sammy Davis, Jr., James Brown, Diana Ross, The Supremes, Gladys Knight & The Pips, Dionne Warwick, The

Jackson 5, Patte LaBelle, Luther Vandross, Stevie Wonder, Aretha Franklin, Mariah Carey, and Lauryn Hill, among others.

The venue declined in the 70s, however, due to crime and drugs prevalent in the neighborhood, and it closed after an 8 year old boy was shot. It was only in 2001 that the interior was renovated and restored, and an exhibit was put forth to celebrate the theater's 75th anniversary. Today, the Apollo Theatre is once again open for business, with Amateur Night taking place every week on Wednesdays.

4. *Radio City Music Hall*

Radio City Music Hall is another unique and magnificent music and entertainment venue in New York City.

The venue was named Radio Corporation of America, one of the first tenants of Rockefeller Complex, and who had also developed studios for NBC at 30 Rockefeller. The somewhat cavernous interior was designed by Edward Durell Stone in austere Art Deco lines. Interior design was by Donald Desky, utilizing geometric Art Deco, and the Great Stage, with its advanced elevators, was designed by Peter Clark and Otis Elevators. It was so advanced that it is said that the U.S. Navy used the same technology for its World War II aircraft carriers.

The various public areas of the Music Hall are also studded with amazing artwork – most created by Depression Era artists. There are also three female nudes cast in aluminum commissioned especially for and displayed variously within the Hall, variously called "Goose Girl" by Robert Laurent, "Eve" by Gwen Lux, and "Spirit of the Dance" by William Zorach. And another notable feature of the Music Hall is its "Mighty Wurlitzer" pipe organ – the largest pipe organ built for a theater.

It took them some time to figure out what type of shows would click with the viewing public. The Music Hall opened in 1932 with a lavish stage show that was not a notable success. In 1933, they shifted to a feature film that included a spectacular stage show. This was their format until 1979, when exclusive film bookings became more difficult in the 70s. After a brief renovation, it opened to the public again in 1980. They still offer movie premieres and feature film presentations, but with a shift in focus to concerts and live stage shows. Each year, the Radio City Christmas Spectacular has become an annual event. Leading artists have performed there in recent years, including televised events such as the Grammy Awards, the MTV Video Music Awards, and the NFL Draft, among others.

This is the largest indoor theater in the world, and performances suffer none the worst for it. Home of the legendary Rockettes, Radio City Hall is the heart of Rockefeller Center – a "palace for the people," with spectacular shows for the average New Yorker. It has the capacity of seating more than 6,000 people, including seats on the pit elevator, and some say with no bad seat in the house. Definitely a place you should visit on a trip to New York.

5. Nitehawk Cinema

© Clay Williams - claywilliamsphoto.com

Want to try something a bit more unique in cinematic venues? Try Nitehawk Cinema in Brooklyn for a unique dinner and movie experience. They call it a dine-in theater, but the term hardly encompasses the Signature Series programming that makes each viewing a unique cinematic experience.

Nitehawk Cinema is a triplex cinema that features large seats with arm rest tables on which you are served food and drinks – and yes, you can have a beer to go with your movie if you so desire. Nitehawk Cinema has set a historical precedent by overturning the prohibition-era liquor law that made serving alcohol in motion picture theaters illegal.

Nitehawk Cinema prides itself on a friendly and neighborhood-like scene in which theater goers can order tasty snacks and craft brews. Everything is done to help ensure a unique cinematic experience – there are films with live music, classics and retrospectives, late shows, brunch screenings, and a specially chosen menu that goes very well with the current film and event. And if that wasn't enough – there is a downstairs café/bar with leather booths, burnished metal and other dark elements.

6. *Brooklyn Bowl*

Another hip venue located in Brooklyn, Brooklyn Bowl is a bowling alley, music venue and restaurant in one.

Brooklyn Bowl is set up in a renovated 1880 ironworks foundry building. It opened to the public in 2009, and has drawn in crowds steadily since then. In 2013, Rolling Stones named it the 20th best music club in America.

If you have a penchant for environmentally-friendly venues, then this will not disappoint, either. Much of the interior design makes use of recycled items such as truck tires (for the concert stage floor), reclaimed glass from the Brooklyn Navy Yard, and wooden floor boards reclaimed from the original ironworks building it is now housed in. It is also lit entirely by LED lights.

There are over two thousand square feet of floor space that includes a 16-lane bowling alley right alongside the music floor. it has a capacity of 600, and the bars serve only draught beers brewed within Brooklyn. Its restaurant is the popular Blue Ribbon, with a seating capacity of 250. It has since opened branches in London and Las Vegas.

Treat yourself to a unique combination of local flavors, distinctive culture, and electrifying live music even when you're bowling. There's no other place quite like it.

7. Lincoln Center for the Performing Arts

The Lincoln Center for the Performing Arts is a complex of buildings housing some of the national and internationally renowned performance arts organizations such as the New York Philharmonic, the Metropolitan Opera, and the New York City Ballet.

Located in Lincoln Square, Manhattan, Lincoln Center was built on the initiative of John D. Rockefeller, Jr, it was part of a Lincoln Square Renewal Project during the 1950s-60s. Lincoln Center became a new cultural hub over the next thirty years.

Lincoln Center originally comprised three buildings: the David Geffen Hall, the David H. Kock Theater, and the Metropolitan Opera House. It has been expanded and renovated since then, and now features 30 indoor and outdoor performance facilities. It is now home to 12 performing arts companies and educational institutions dedicated to the music, dance and drama. It is now the world's leading venue and presenter of the performing arts. In 2009, Lincoln Center celebrated their 50th anniversary.

Over 400 diverse performances are offered each year – from music, opera, theater, dance, and other events that will surely satisfy any appetite. There is even outdoor dancing to live music at the Josie Robertson Plaza.

Check out their upcoming scheduled performances too see if there is anything you'd like to see. Chances are, there will be!

8. Carnegie Hall

Deemed the preeminent concert hall in the world, Carnegie Hall has set the standard with performances from outstanding musical artists, great popular musicians, and other world figures since it first opened in 1891. It is located at 881 Seventh Avenue in Midtown Manhattan.

Carnegie Hall features three auditoriums with a total seating capacity of 3, 671. Its building is one of the last large buildings in New York that was built entirely of masonry, without a steel frame – though a steel frame was erected around segments of the building when several flights of studio spaces were added near the turn of the 20th century. The exterior is a pleasant rendering of narrow Roman bricks of mellow ochre, with details in terracotta and brownstone. A beautiful but wonderfully understated architectural construction and design.

Whether you are an aficionado of jazz, folk, orchestral concerts, chamber music, or other popular or world music, a performance in Carnegie Hall symbolizes the emblem of musical achievement. Some of the greats have performed here – Tchaikovsky, Horowitz, Bernstein, even The Beatles and Judy Garland.

9. *Tour New York City by Night*

You will have to exercise some discretion in choosing which tours to join for a night time trek through New York City. It pretty much depends on what you want to see –

there are bus tours, ferry tours, walking tours, museum by night tours, or viewing the Manhattan skyline by night tours. There are some that even offer night helicopter tours. If you're lucky, you can find a tour that offers more than one of these options in one package.

Touted as the "City that Never Sleeps," you might wonder just how different New York City is at night compared to how it is during the day. Not so different in certain respects, perhaps – the bustle and crowds will still be there in some central locations such as Times Square. In other areas, it will be completely different as the Financial District has often been referred to as being a kind of ghost town when the sun comes down and the businessmen and women go home.

What does inspire a breathtaking view is the City Skyline – a view best appreciated from either a nighttime ferry tour or a nighttime excursion up to a viewing deck in one of several observation decks in the various towering skyscrapers of the city.

Some people, however, prefer a simple walking tour of the City – an exploration of one of the most visited cities in the world under the lights of many of the surrounding billboards and buildings. If you find a reputable and professional guided tour, it is sure to be a memorable tour –

definitely one to fit into your schedule during a New York City vacation.

10.NYC bar scene

Check out New York City's bar scene – and there are plenty to choose from. Whether you wish to join a pub crawl, a nightclub tour, or just want to look for a great watering hole that might feature great live music or stand-up comedians, New York by night is a great way to explore New York City's night life.

Don't know where to start? A well-guided tour is sure to bring you to the best picks in the city, while also providing a level of security in having a guide ready to hand. If you are the more solitary type, however, and prefer to have your drinks with one or two friends instead of a group, here are a few recommended bars to choose from. This does not necessarily exclude others, of course. The lively New York City bar scene is so thriving that it is difficult to choose – or to make a recommendation. What we are giving you here, therefore, is a starting point upon which you can begin your adventures:

- Black Tail at Battery Park – they offer live music twice a week
- Super Power at Crown Heights – budget friendly with great cocktails
- As Is NYC at Hell's Kitchen – rotating draft beers and gourmet bar food!
- Mr. Purple at the Lower East Side – located at the 15th floor of Hotel Indigo at the Lower East Side, great views and expansive terraces. They even have a pool!
- Belle Shoals in Williamsburg – Souther style bar with an outdoor patio and live music on Thursdays and Fridays.
- Seaborne at the Red Hook – for cocktails, frozen drinks, with booths that come with self-serve water taps.
- Proletariat at the East Village – clandestine and unusual, with some obscure but tasty drafts
- Dead Rabbit Grocery and Grog Shop at the Financial District – yep, bankers killed the rabbit. Well, not

really. A great environment and a staggering bar collection.

- Barcade at Williamsburg – a chance to drink beer and play arcade games.

Remember though, that if you want to spend your night dancing, you must look for a club. Yes, there's wonderful music at the bar you went to, but New York City's Cabaret Laws regulate dancing only to certain clubs. Sound stupid? We'll leave it to you to decide. Follow the rules, anyway, be safe, and you'll have a hassle-free and enjoyable vacation. After all, you can still dance freely – as long as you do it in the right place. Want some suggestions? Here are a few:

- Output at Williamsburg
- Black Flamingo at Williamsburg
- Good Room at Greenpoint
- 1 Oak near Tenth Avenue
- The Lively near 13th Street, at Ninth Ave.
- Bossa Nova Civic Club at Bushwick
- Flash Factory at 28th Stret, Seventh Avenue

Chapter Nine: Off New York City's Beaten Path

Sometimes you find the most amazing discoveries by going down the road less traveled. New York City is now one of the most popular tourist destinations in the world, with the best tourist spots literally drawing crowds. But as is true in every city or locality – there are always hidden gems still waiting to be discovered. Maybe they are not quite so popular as some of the more flashy tourist spots in the City, but they are no less interesting for it.

Below we give you some of the lesser-known spots of interest within New York City - many of them providing unique perspective and interesting history that lends a richer color to the city that is New York.

1. Doyers Street and the Bloody Angle

At the heart of Chinatown in Manhattan is a 200 ft long street that branches off from Pell Street, running south then southeast to the intersection of Bowery, Chatham Square, and Division Street. This is Doyers Street, nicknamed "the Bloody Angle" back in the 1930s.

Doyers Street is pretty much a typical street in Chinatown – lined with several shops including a restaurant, barber shop, hairstylists, and a branch of the US postal service. The street was named for Hendrik Doyer, a Dutch immigrant who used to operate a distillery here in 1791. There is also a Tea Parlor, a Gift Shop, and what used to be the first Chinese language theater that operated from 1893-1911.

The one distinguishing feature about this street is that it curves sharply somewhere in the middle. It has been hypothesized that the street follows the curve of the narrow old cart path that was in use during Doyers' time.

Doyers Street was nicknamed "the Bloody Angle" back in the 1930s because it was the site of numerous shootings and killings among the Tong Gangs of Chinatown. The term "hatchet man" derives from these incidents, as hatchets were often used in violent deaths that took place at this street – more than at any other street intersection in the United States, according to law enforcement officials at the time.

While Doyers Street was relatively peaceful, on the night of August 7, 1905, there arose a confrontation between the Hip Sing and the On Leong Tong gangsters while they were inside the theater watching a play entitled The King's Daughter. Several Hip Sing members fired into a crowd that numbered some 500 Chinamen, and they just kept on firing. Afterwards, they slipped out using one of many underground tunnels that branched out from Doyers Street.

This incident kicked off a Tong war that lasted for years – most of the confrontations taking place at the bend on Doyers Street. And the blind corner created by the sharp bend on Doyers Street created a great ambush position, leaving bloody victims with their blood soaking into the street of the bloody angle, while the gangsters escaped via the underground tunnels. After years of bloody killings and violence, a kind of peace was finally achieved in 1913, but it didn't last.

In 1989, during what people call the most violent decade of New York City, a new war erupted between two different rival gangs – the Chinese Flying Dragons, and the Vietnamese BTK (Born to Kill). This time around, it was far more ruthless. Even the Chinese gangs were scared of the Vietnamese – young men relocated from Saigon during the Vietnam War.

Quiet came to the Bloody Angle only in 1994, when most of the illegal gambling dens along Doyers Street had been essentially driven off, and the gangs no longer had any business interests to fight for. And the leader of the Hip Sings had fallen into ill health.

Today, Doyers Street have been taken over by small shops and business concerns, and even the underground tunnels are lined with various shops and offices – a more respectable façade being drawn over the bloody history of the street due to ever-increasing gentrification. Tours are now being offered visitors into this heart of Chinatown, with stories of the bloody conflict that once took over the street.

2. *Berlin Wall segments*

The Berlin Wall – which once isolated West Berlin until it was completely demolished in 1992 – were actually divided into segments and given to various institutions all over the world. Five of these segments are now scattered in various locations throughout New York City:

- 520 Madison Avenue, Midtown Manhattan
- Kowsky Plaza, Battery Park, Manhattan
- The United Nations, Murray Hill, Manhattan
- Ripley's Believe it or Not, Times Square, Manhattan
- The Intrepid Museum, Hell's Kitchen, Manhattan

The distinctive art-graffiti that covered the Wall was started by artist Thierry Noir, who began painting a section of the wall closest to his apartment in order to make it less menacing. Soon other artists joined, in, and the 14-foot tall ostensibly designed to protect the Eastern Block from fascist elements, but which actually served to prevent the mass emigration and defection of the East German population and resulting brain drain after World War II, had become a 14-foot tall canvas.

A magnificent graphical representation of the sordid events that took place near these walls before they were demolished – especially considering that these thick walls overlaid with artistic graffiti were once topped with guard towers and the surrounding area around these towers were once called the "death strip." A great memento of how the East Germans eventually won their freedom.

3. *Renwick Smallpox Hospital*

Dark and dreary, with a distinctive menacing air, and reputed to be dangerous and haunted – the Smallpox Hospital on Roosevelt Island in Manhattan is a frightening sight that nobody today would ever willingly go near – especially at night.

Sometimes called the Renwick Smallpox Hospital for its architect James Renwick, Jr., then later on as the Maternity and Charity Hospital Training School, the 100-bed, Gothic Revival style hospital first opened in 1856, in an otherwise undeloped southern area of what used to be referred to as Blackwell's Island.

The ruins mark the period of New York history when large outbreaks of smallpox affected the population. Despite the availability of the smallpox vaccine, the arrival of infected immigrants, the disease was difficult to address. The hospital was thus located in a somewhat isolated area for quarantine purposes.

Later on, in 1875, the hospital closed and the place became a training center for nurses of the City Hospital. As many of the structures fell into disrepair and became obsolete, the Charity Hospital and Nurses' school were closed, their operations being moved to Queens. The buildings fell into disrepair until the only word that can be used to describe them now would be "ruins." It was listed in the National Register of Historic Places in 1972 and designated a New York City landmark four years later.

At present, there is an ongoing $4.5 million stabilization project for the structure, after which there are plans to open the Smallpox Hospital to the public as the centerpiece of a new Southpoint Park on the island.

4. IRT Lexington Avenue Line – City Hall

The original southern terminal station of the first line of the New York City terminal was located underneath a public area in front of City Hall and was opened to the public as far back as 1904. Its services, however, were discontinued in 1945 due to several factors: having been built on a curve, it could only accommodate five-car trains, which was inefficient when the numbers of subway passengers grew, and because of its proximity to the Brooklyn Bridge Station.

It has still been active as a turnaround for the 6 line, but now the New York Transit Museum is providing the public with a new perspective on this amazing subway terminal through exclusive guided tours. As of this writing, tickets cost $50 per person, and usually sell out very quickly.

Many easily consider this a worthwhile trip – the subway was constructed in a stunning Romanesque Revival style that features a mezzanine area above the platform, tall tile arches, brass fixtures, chandeliers, skylights, polychrome tile, and elegant curves. Wrought iron chandeliers and three skylights of cut amethyst glass provided natural lighting onto parts of the platform. It has been remarkably well preserved, compared to other subway stations of the time.

Remember that attendance requires prior membership to the New York Transit Museum. Tours are generally offered some 16 times a year to around 40 people at a time. A great way to relive the beginnings of New York City's subway system!

5. Blockhouse Number One

There is a small fort located in the northern part of Central Park in Manhattan, and people commonly refer to it simply as "The Blockhouse." It is estimated to be the second oldest structure in the park, after Cleopatra's Needle.

Built in 1814, the Blockhouse was part of a series of fortifications in northern Manhattan and Morningside Heights (formerly called Harlem Heights) during the Revolutionary War. Based on trial excavations in 1995, however, it was discovered that the Blockhouse was actually built on a much older structure. Its foundations have been found to date back to the time of the British occupation of Manhattan.

The features of the Blockhouse include a two-story bunker with a small staircase around a small area where a wooden platform would have once stood. This would have included a revolving turret for a cannon, with small gunports at the sides.

The fort was thereafter used as an ammunition and storage building, and for this purpose, the structure was fortified by the addition of at least two feet of stone work. Later on, near the turn of the 20th century, the current entrance, a staircase, and a tall flagpole was added.

The location of the Blockhouse within Central Park is not that easy to reach – it is situation in a wooded area that is rugged and high. Once you gain access to its immediate area, however, you get a great vantage point of Harlem Meer. The interior of structure is not open to the public, although the Urban Park Rangers do give occasional tours. In general, the doors are securely closed by a large metal gate.

6. *The Irish Hunger Memorial*

Situated at Battery Park, Mahattan, the Irish Hunger Memorial was designed to commemorate and to raise awareness regarding the Great Irish Famine which killed over a million people in Ireland from 1845 to 1852.

The memorial was designed to capture the atmosphere of a blighted Irish landscape – complete with stones, soil and native vegetation which were transported from the western coast of Ireland for this purpose. There is also a reconstruction of an authentic Irish cottage dating back from the 19th century – donated by the Slack family who once lived there and then eventually abandoning it in the 1960s.

The Memorial also features "Outfall, 2015" – a sculpture was a computer-generated scale model of Mount Peechee, and intended to represent the glacial origin of the Bow River.

The entire memorial is not only a reminder of the past, but also a reminder to us of the ravages of hunger and of its connection to poverty and our access to land.

7. Staten Island Boat Graveyard

Ever wonder where boats go when they die? At least for the remnants of the New York City shipping industry, there is a handy Boat Graveyard in the Arthur Kill in Rossville, near the Fresh Kills Landfill on the northern shore of Staten Island. It is the official dumping ground for old and wrecked boats, tugboats, barges, and ferries.

Sometimes called the Witte Marine Scrapyard, the Arthur Kill Board Yard, or the Tugboat Graveyard, it was officially named the Donjon Iron and Metal Scrap Processing Facility in 2014. Not quite as romantic, yes, which is probably why the old names still stick.

The scrapyard began in the 1930s by owner John Witte. Essentially a scrapyard like any other, the useful components are salvaged and boat parts sold. But because it has been in operation for so long, it has involuntarily become a shipyard museum, with over 100 ships with dates from all throughout the 20th century.

The place has become a tourist attraction, even with the No Trespassing signs. People navigate their way through the hulking metal and rotting ships, riding on boats or kayaks, and photographers and artists have made a great subject of the eerie graveyard's eerie environment.

8. Atlantic Avenue Subway Tunnel

Also called the Cobble Hill Tunnel, the Atlantic Avenue Tunnel is the world's oldest subway tunnel. It was built in 1844 underneath a busy Brooklyn Street, runs for a half-mile long, and accommodated two standard gauge railroad tracks.

Records show that the tunnel's construction was rooted in the growing number of accidents that resulted from pedestrians and carriages and the Long Island Railroad train all sharing the same road. Cornelius Vanderilt really wanted to make sure that his trains were not delayed – and delays came often because of the continuous accidents aboveground. So he decided to build the world's first underground train system.

One interesting legend is that of murder. Irish workers were supposedly told by the British contractor that they would have to work on Sunday and miss church. In their anger, one of the men pulled out a gun and shot him. They then buried his body behind the wall, where it remains concealed to this day.

It was rediscovered again in 1980, by Bob Diamond who was then a 19 year old engineering student. His discovery was the result of sheer persistence and some amazing detective work through old maps and documents. He finally did find the tunnel. Because of his amazing discovery and tenacity in locating the old Atlantic Avenue Subway Tunnel, he was put in charge of it, and he formed The Brooklyn Historic Railway Association preserve, publicize, and provide public access to the tunnel. BHRA now conducts tours and events within the Atlantic Avenue Tunnel.

Neither is Bob Diamond done, yet. Someday, he hopes to open up the end of the tunnel which he hopes may actually contain an old locomotive. At least 6 blocks of the tunnel are still sealed off by a wall of dirt. Who knows? Maybe he's right again.

9. Hell Gate Bridge

Hell Gate Bridge is a steel-through arch railroad bridge that spans Hell's Gate – a strait on the East River, between Astoria, Queens, and what used to be the separate islands of Randall's and Wards, which are now connected by landfill.

The term Hell Gate for the narrow strait in the East River derives from Dutch "Hellegat" which means "bright strait" or "clear opening." It was hardly a clear opening – its current name "Hell Gate" actually seems more appropriate for the actual conditions of the waters – with converging tide-driven currents, a giant whirlpool, and rocks, reefs and islands, navigation is hazardous, to say the least. Perhaps it is because of this that the anglicized version of the name "Hell Gate" stuck.

Navigating through these waters were so dangerous that by the 1850s, one in fifty ships were either damaged or sunk, and an average of 1,000 ships running aground in the strait.

Hell Gate Bridge was intended to link New York and New England. It was designed by Gustav Lindenthal, whose calculations were so precise that the final adjustment needed when everything was lifted into place was only 5/16 inches, or 7.9 mm. Construction finished in 1916, and the bridge was opened to rail traffic in March 1917. At the time of its construction, it was the longest steel arch bridge in the world. It became a vital connection between New York and New England, and served international engineers all over the world. By the end of 1968, however, and due to the rise of the automobile, use of the railway dwindled, and use of the bridge itself dwindled.

There was an effort to repair the bridge in 1991 – but because of a flaw in the paint formula, it resulted in a reddish faded appearance that people jokingly referred to as "Hell Gate Red."

The bridge's construction was so solid that it was noted in a 2005 issue of Discovery magazine that it would be the last New York bridge to collapse if humans disappeared, and it would still take a millennium to do so. Most other bridges would fall in 30 years. It is one of New York City's more unappreciated and unacknowledged bridges.

10. Trinity Church Cemetery

The Episcopal Parish of Trinity Church in Lower Manhattan actually has three burial grounds in the City, including at St. Paul's and Trinity Cemetery in Washington Heights – which were established when the church began to run out of space in its own churchyard.

The burial grounds have been in use since they opened in 1697. Some of the graves here date back to the 17th century, and contain some of the city's oldest carved tombstones – including an ominous cryptogram. The oldest tombstone here is that or Richard Churcher, a five year old boy who died in 1681. The entire cemetery carries with it a wealth of 17th-18th century symbolism, and beautiful, if somewhat eerie, landscaping.

Some of the notables buried here include Alexander Hamilton, William Bradford, Robert Fulton, Captain James Lawrence, and Albert Gallatin.

Chapter Ten: Conclusion

How your visit to New York City ultimately turns out depends to a large extent on what side of it you want to see. As you can probably tell from the selections we have provided you in this book – the choices are plenty, and amazingly diverse. Whether you choose to immerse yourself in historical sights, artistic displays and museums, the many artistic and musical performances in the City, or simply to go shopping and food tripping, New York City has you covered. This is a place to experience life in a way that you won't be able to anywhere else – the cultural and ethnic mix of the New York City population, including the unique history of the city, and its preeminent role in the nation's cultural, artistic, and architectural progress as a whole has yielded a City that is beautiful for its diversity and for its sheer grandeur just as much as its seedy and dark side.

The lists of things to see and do in this book are by no means exhaustive. Allow yourself to explore when you can, be open to surprises, though plan your trip carefully. And as always, stay safe. Here are a few tips to keep in mind as you make your preparations for a New York City trip:

- For international travelers, make copies and backups of your passport and credit card information and store them in a safe place - should your cards get stolen or lost, it's always a good idea to have copies of them for cancellations or new applications.
- Plan your itinerary beforehand - not only does this allow you to choose the most convenient hotel, and figure out how to get from one point to another, but it will also allow you to make the most of your trip. That said, don't discount or ignore the occasional pleasant surprise that often does happens during travels.
- Pack the essentials: a small medical kit, especially if you're prone to an illness or two, snack bags, universal chargers and plug adapters, folding bags for packing souvenirs and other stuff you might pick up at the local markets, and digital gear to help you

store your memories. Try not to pack too much gear, however - nor ones that are too bulky.

- Budget yourself well. Prices will generally not be cheap in New York City, and you'll find yourself dropping some serious dough during your shopping trips. Keep in mind how much you can afford, however, and stay within your budget. If you can't really splurge, there are plenty of smaller and cheaper shops to explore, with products that are just as good – if without the designer labels. If you are on a budget – try to get a tourist pass to save on tickets for the major attractions. You might find reduced admission fees or freebies being offered by certain places of interest. Take advantage! If you do plan on making use of the subway during your visit, it's also probably a good idea to buy a subway pass.

- If you're planning on watching a Broadway show, concert, or even an NBA game, please do make your reservations early. The same goes for a planned dinner in a popular restaurant. With the millions of people now living in New York, you'll have to remember to stay on your toes if you want to beat the crowds.

- Always be prepared to walk – so pack comfortable, walking or running shoes. The dense population of

New York will begin to crowd at some point – and especially if you are heading to popular tourist spots, you can probably expect to get stuck in a crowd at one point or another. Be kind to your feet and wear sensible footwear. As an alternative, you can try to get around the city on a bike instead. There are plenty of cycling routes around Manhattan – just remember to be safe, wear a helmet, and stick to the lanes.

- Don't forget that New York City isn't just Manhattan. There are just as many interesting sights to see – and cheaper places to shop and dine – in New York City's other boroughs.
- Budget your time well, too – it is far too easy to get stuck in one interesting museum for an entire afternoon, and not be able to see any of the other sights you had planned for that day. Explore based on what you really want to see – scheduling might seem like overkill, but it is a good idea. You don't want to end your vacation hardly having seen even half of the things on your list.
- Practice the general rules of safety. New York City is safe, as a general rule - but that doesn't mean you should push against its limits, either. Use your common sense. Don't do drugs; don't drink if you're

underage, and get good insurance coverage that you will be able to use in New York City hospitals.

New York City Quick Travel Guide

1. *New York City Quick Facts*
    a. Currency – US Dollar ($/USD)
    b. Primary Language spoken: English
    c. Weather and seasons – humid subtropical climate, with an average of 57% of annual sunshine
        - Spring – unpredictable and can range from chilly to warm, to hot and humid, though generally mild with low humidity
        - Summer – typically warm to hot and humid, with a daily mean temperature

of 76.5 degrees Fahrenheit (24.7 degrees Celsius)

- Autumn - unpredictable and can range from chilly to warm, to hot and humid, though generally mild with low humidity
- Winter – cold and damp, with the coldest temperatures in January; average mean temperature is at 32.6 degrees Fahrenheit (0.3 degrees Celsius) but can drop to 10 degrees Fahrenheing (-12 degrees Celsius)

d. Tourist seasons – no clear "peak" tourist season, so prices are pretty steady year-round

2. *Transportation*

a. Rapid Transit Lines
   i. New York City Subway
   ii. Buses and an intercity bus terminal

b. Aviation
   i. JFK International Airport
   ii. Newark Liberty International Airport
   iii. La Guardia Airport

c. Ferries

d. Taxis

e. Aerial Tramway between Roosevelt and Manhattan Islands

f. River Crossings through bridges or tunnels

Getting Around Within New York City

- Subway
- Bus
- Cycling
- Ferries
- By Car
- By Cab
- Walking

Index

A

B

C

D

E

F

M

N

O

P

Q

R

S

T

U

W

Y

Photo References

Page 1 Photo by Derek Jensen (Tysto) via Wikimedia Commons. <https://commons.wikimedia.org/wiki/File:Liberty-statue-with-manhattan.jpg>

Page 11 Photo by LWYang from USA via Wikimedia Commons. <https://commons.wikimedia.org/wiki/File:Park_Av_looking_south_in_Midtown_Manhattan.jpg>

Page 13 Photo by Alex Maisuradze via Wikimedia Commons. <https://commons.wikimedia.org/wiki/File:Upper_East_Side_NYC.jpg>

Page 14 Photo by Andreas Praefcke via Wikimedia Commons. <https://commons.wikimedia.org/wiki/File:NYC_SoHo_Green_Street.jpg>

Page 16 Photo by Beyond My Ken via Wikimedia Commons. <https://commons.wikimedia.org/wiki/File:264-266_West_25th_Street.jpg>

Page 17 Photo by 7mike5000 via Wikimedia Commons. <https://commons.wikimedia.org/wiki/File:Madison_Street-Manhattan_looking_south.jpg>

Page 19 Photo by JJBers via Wikimedia Commons. <https://commons.wikimedia.org/wiki/File:Flatiron_District_Skyline_8-1-2012.jpg>

Page 20 Photo by Jim Henderson via Wikimedia Commons. <https://commons.wikimedia.org/wiki/File:Allen-Delancey_Mall_jeh.JPG>

Page 22 Photo by Seth Werkheiser from Brooklyn, NY, USA via Wikimedia Commons. <https://commons.wikimedia.org/wiki/File:Greenwich_Village_2005.jpg>

Page 23 Photo by peterwasef0 via Pixabay. <https://pixabay.com/en/usa-brooklyn-america-644951/>

Page 24 Photo by Jleon via Wikimedia Commons <https://commons.m.wikimedia.org/wiki/File:NYC_Jackson_Heights_3.jpg>

Page 27 Photo by Balou46 via Wikimedia Commons. <https://commons.wikimedia.org/wiki/File:NYC-manhattan-rockefeller-01.jpg>

Page 29 Photo by Fletcher6 via Wikimedia Commons. <https://commons.wikimedia.org/wiki/File:Apple_Store_Fifth_Avenue.jpg>

Page 31 Photo by Gryffindor via Wikimedia Commons. <https://commons.wikimedia.org/wiki/File:South_Street_Seaport_005.JPG>

Page 33 Photo by Alexisrael via Wikimedia Commons. <https://commons.wikimedia.org/wiki/File:Little_Italy_NY_Street.JPG>

Page 35 Photo by Ian Gratton via Wikimedia Commons. <https://commons.wikimedia.org/wiki/File:Macy%27s_Department_store_Herald_Square_(8403806690).jpg>

Page 37 Photo by Leif Knutsen via Wikimedia Commons. https://commons.wikimedia.org/wiki/File:Madison_Ave_NYC_looking_nor.jpg

Page 39 Photo by LWYang via Wikimedia Commons. <https://commons.wikimedia.org/wiki/File:N_7_St_Bedford_Av_Williamsburg.jpg>

Page 40 Photo by Gryffindor via Wikimedia Commons. <https://commons.wikimedia.org/wiki/File:Chelsea_Market_IMG_9034.JPG>

Page 41 Photo by Sheynhertz-Unbayg via Wikimedia Commons. <https://commons.wikimedia.org/wiki/File:Orchard_St_looking_south_at_Rivington_St.jpg>

Page 43 Photo by Evanscott7 via Wikimedia Commons. <https://en.wikipedia.org/wiki/File:Brooklyn_Flea_Skylight_One_Hanson.jpg>

Page 46 Photo by Arad via Wikimedia Commons. <https://commons.wikimedia.org/wiki/File:Metropolitan_Museum_of_Art_entrance_NYC.JPG>

Page 48 Photo by Gautier Poupeau via Wikimedia Commons. <https://commons.wikimedia.org/wiki/File:Cloister%27s_Museum_(4849206361).jpg>

Page 50 Photo by Ingfbruno via Wikimedia Commons. <https://commons.wikimedia.org/wiki/File:USA-NYC-American_Museum_of_Natural_History.JPG>

Page 51 Photo by Jim Henderson via Wikimedia Commons. <https://commons.wikimedia.org/wiki/File:Tenement_Museum_Orchard_%26_Houston_corner_shop_jeh.jpg>

Page 53 Photo by Alsandro via Wikimedia Commons. <https://commons.wikimedia.org/wiki/File:MOMAyard.JPG>

Page 55 Photo by Gryffindor via Wikimedia Commons. <https://commons.wikimedia.org/wiki/File:Henry_C_Frick_House_009.JPG>

Page 57 Photo by Nightscream via Wikimedia Commons. <https://commons.wikimedia.org/wiki/File:12.6.11National9-11MemorialByLuigiNovi4.jpg>y

Page 59 Photo by Beyond My Ken via Wikimedia Commons. <https://commons.wikimedia.org/wiki/File:Museum_of_the_City_of_New_York_1220_Fifth_Avenue_from_north.jpg>

Page 60 Photo by Elisa.rolle via Wikimedia Commons. <https://commons.wikimedia.org/wiki/File:Pierpont_Morgan_Library.jpg>

Page 62 Photo by GK tramrunner via Wikimedia Commons. <https://commons.wikimedia.org/wiki/File:EldridgeStreetSynagogue.jpg>

Page 66 Photo by Derek Jensen (Tysto) via Wikimedia Commons. <https://commons.wikimedia.org/wiki/File:Liberty-statue-from-front.jpg>

Page 69 Photo by Afshin Darian via Wikimedia Commons. <https://commons.wikimedia.org/wiki/File:Castle_Clinton,_Battery_Park.jpg>

Page 71 Photo by Beyond My Ken via Wikimedia Commons. <https://commons.wikimedia.org/wiki/File:Theodore_Roosevelt_Birthplace.jpg?fastcci_from=11137227&c1=11137227&d1=15&s=200&a=list >

Page 73 Photo by PAT M IN NYC from Wikis Take Manhattan 2009 via Wikimedia Commons. <https://commons.wikimedia.org/wiki/File:WTM3_PAT_M_IN_NYC_0027.jpg>

Page 75 Photo by Beyond My Ken via Wikimedia Commons. <https://commons.wikimedia.org/wiki/File:2015_Green-Wood_Cemetery_Gate_from_inside_with_gate_house.jpg>)

Page 78 Photo by Matias Garabedian via Wikimedia Commons. <https://commons.wikimedia.org/wiki/File:Grand_Central_Terminal_(9074218008).jpg>

Page 80 Photo by Norbert Nagel, Morfelden-Walldorf, Germany via Wikimedia Commons. <https://commons.wikimedia.org/wiki/File:New_York_City_Ellis_Island_03.jpg>

Page 83 Photo by John Cunniff from New York, USA via Wikimedia Commons. <https://commons.wikimedia.org/wiki/File:Brooklyn_Bridge_and_One_World_Trade_Center,_morning_light_(20887439332).jpg>

Page 85 Photo by Elisa.rolle via Wikimedia Commons. <https://commons.wikimedia.org/wiki/File:New_York_Public_Library_(1).JPG>

Page 87 Photo by Jean-Christophe BENOIST via Wikimedia Commons. <https://commons.wikimedia.org/wiki/File:NYC_-_St._Patrick%27s_Cathedral_-_Facade.jpg>

Page 92 Photo by Terabass via Wikimedia Commons. <https://commons.wikimedia.org/wiki/File:New_york_times_square-terabass.jpg>

Page 95 Photo by Kcpwiki via Wikimedia Commons. <https://commons.wikimedia.org/wiki/File:Vista_of_Great_Lawn_from_Belvedere_Castle.jpg>

Page 98 Photo by Smithfl via Wikimedia Commons. <https://commons.wikimedia.org/wiki/File:Empirestatebuildingfrombrooklynnewyork.jpg>

Page 101 Photo by Jean-Christophe BENOIST via Wikimedia Commons. <https://commons.wikimedia.org/wiki/File:NYC_-_Washington_Square_Park_-_Arch.jpg>

Page 103 Photo by Misterweiss via Wikimedia Commons. <https://commons.wikimedia.org/wiki/File:Chrysler_Building_2005_3.jpg>

Page 105 Photo by MusikAnimal via Wikimedia Commons. <https://commons.wikimedia.org/wiki/File:Federal_Hall_and_George_Washington_statue_in_New_York_City.JPG>

Page 108 Photo by Daniel Case via Wikimedia Commons. <https://commons.wikimedia.org/wiki/File:Audience_watching_musicians_perform_on_High_Line.jpg>

Page 110 Photo by Jean-Christophe BENOIST via Wikimedia Commons. <https://commons.wikimedia.org/wiki/File:New-York_-_Bryant_Park.jpg>

Page 112 Photo by InSapphoWeTrust via Wikimedia Commons. <https://commons.wikimedia.org/wiki/File:Staten_Island_Ferry_"Spirit_of_America"_(7208224768).jpg>

Page 113 Photo by Richiebits via Wikimedia Commons. <https://commons.wikimedia.org/wiki/File:BBGJapaneseHillPondGarden.jpg>

Page 115 Photo by Bloodyrich via Wikimedia Commons. <https://commons.wikimedia.org/wiki/File:Theateroutsidepub.jpg>

Page 117 Photo by Patrick Kwan via Wikimedia Commons. <https://commons.wikimedia.org/wiki/File:Dragon_in_Chinatown_NYC_Lunar_New_Year.jpg>

Page 119 Photo by Tony Fischer via Wikimedia Commons. <https://commons.wikimedia.org/wiki/File:The_Midway,_Coney_Island,_Night_View,_From_the_Wonder_Wheel_(3897789133).jpg>

Page 121 Photo by dronepicr via Wikimedia Commons. <https://commons.wikimedia.org/wiki/File:New_York_Yankees_Stadion_(22037226108).jpg>

Page 123 Photo by Postdlf from w via Wikimedia Commons. <https://commons.wikimedia.org/wiki/File:Bronx_Zoo_001.jpg>

Page 125 Photo by Bin im Garten via Wikimedia Commons. <https://commons.wikimedia.org/wiki/File:New_York_City_Mai_2009_PD_021.JPG>

Page 126 Photo by AEMoreira042281 via Wikimedia Commons. <https://commons.wikimedia.org/wiki/File:Barclays_Center_western_side.jpg>

Page 128 Photo by Jim Henderson via Wikimedia Commons. <https://commons.wikimedia.org/wiki/File:El-Rawsheh_Cafe_%26_Restaurant_Steinway_St_jeh.jpg>

Page 130 Photo by Jorge Royan via Wikimedia Commons. <https://commons.wikimedia.org/wiki/File:NYC_-_Madame_Tussaud%27s_-_1845.jpg>

Page 132 Photo by Lapizzaria via Wikimedia Commons. <https://commons.wikimedia.org/wiki/File:NYPizzaWindow.jpg>

Page 136 Photo by Tony from Commons: Wikipedia Takes Manhattan Project of April 4, 2008 via Wikimedia Commons. <https://commons.wikimedia.org/wiki/File:WTM_tony_0083.jpg>

Page 138 Photo by Andreas Praefcke via Wikimedia Commons. <https://commons.wikimedia.org/wiki/File:Ambassador_Theatre_NYC.jpg>

Page 140 Photo by The All-Nite Images from NY, USA via Wikimedia Commons. <https://commons.wikimedia.org/wiki/File:Apollo_sign_3.jpg>

Page 142 Photo by Pete Stewart from Perth, Australia via Wikimedia Commons. <https://commons.wikimedia.org/wiki/File:Flickr_-_Shinrya_-_Radio_City_NYC.jpg>

Page 145 Photo by Emily C via Flickr. <https://www.flickr.com/photos/603to212/7774726002/>

Page 147 Photo by Jim.henderson via Wikimedia Commons. <https://commons.wikimedia.org/wiki/File:Brooklyn_Bowl_bar_61_Wythe_Av_jeh.jpg>

Page 149 Photo by Robert Mintzes via Wikimedia Commons. <https://commons.wikimedia.org/wiki/File:Lincoln_Center_Main.jpg>

Page 151 Photo by Simeon87 via Wikimedia Commons. <https://commons.wikimedia.org/wiki/File:Carnegie_Hall_2008.JPG>

Page 152 Photo by OscarUrdaneta via Wikimedia Commons. <https://commons.wikimedia.org/wiki/File:New_York_Skylines_19.JPG>

Page 154 Photo by Kenny Louie from Vancouver, Canada. <https://commons.wikimedia.org/wiki/File:NYC_TAXI_(7038011669).jpg>

Page 158 Photo by Beyond My Ken via Wikimedia Commons. <https://commons.wikimedia.org/wiki/File:Doyers_Street_Chinatown.jpg>

Page 161 Photo by Ronny-Bonny via Wikimedia Commons. <https://commons.wikimedia.org/wiki/File:Segment_of_Berlin_wall_in_New_York_City.jpg>

Page 162 Photo by Earnest B via Wikimedia Commons. <https://commons.wikimedia.org/wiki/File:New-York-City,-Roosevelt-Island,-Smallpox-Hospital,-Eingangsfront-(1996)_crop.jpg>

Page 164 Photo by Julian Dunn from New York, USA via Wikimedia Commons. <https://commons.wikimedia.org/wiki/File:City_Hall_ceiling_vc.jpg>

Page 166 Photo by Гатерас via Wikimedia Commons. <https://commons.wikimedia.org/wiki/File:Blockhouse_New_York_entrance.JPG>

Page 168 Photo by Catson via Wikimedia Commons. <https://commons.wikimedia.org/wiki/File:Cottage_ruins.jpg >

Page 169 Photo by U.S. National Archives and Records Administration via Wikimedia Commons. <https://commons.wikimedia.org/wiki/File:VIEW_FROM_CARTERET,_NJ,_ACROSS_THE_ARTHUR_KILL_TO_

STATEN_ISLAND_SCRAPYARD_AND_SHIP_GRAVEYARD_-_NARA_-_551997.jpg >

Page 171 Photo by Vlad Rud via Wikimedia Commons. <https://commons.wikimedia.org/wiki/File:Atlantic_Ave_Tunnel.jpg>

Page 173 Photo by Ben Schumin via Wikimedia Commons. <https://commons.wikimedia.org/wiki/File:Hell_Gate_Bridge_from_Acela.jpg>

Page 174 Photo by Gryffindor via Wikimedia Commons. <https://commons.wikimedia.org/wiki/File:Trinity_Church_Cemetery_NYC_9109.JPG >

Page 177 Photo by Daniel Schwen via Wikimedia Commons. <https://commons.wikimedia.org/wiki/File:NYC_wideangle_south_from_Top_of_the_Rock.jpg >

Page 183 Photo by Michael Danser via Wikimedia Commons. <https://commons.wikimedia.org/wiki/File:Toys%27R%27Us_store_in_Time_Square,_NYC_2005.jpg>

References

"10 Best Things to Do in Williamsburg." Ellen Freudenheim. <http://brooklyn.about.com/od/eventsthingstodo/tp/10-Best-Things-To-Do-In-Williamsburg-Brooklyn.htm>

"10 Hottest Bars in NYC." Zagat. <https://www.zagat.com/l/new-york-city/the-10-hottest-bars-in-nyc>

"10 Reasons to Visit a Museum." KYOB. <http://colleendilen.com/2009/07/31/10-reasons-to-visit-a-museum/>

"15 Top-Rated Tourist Attractions in New York City." Lana Law. <http://www.planetware.com/tourist-attractions-/new-york-city-us-ny-nyc.htm>

"17 Secret Places in NYC You Didn't Know About (But Should)." Austin Bradley. <http://julep.triplemint.com/17-secret-places-in-nyc-you-didnt-know-about-but-should/>

"20 Hidden Gems To Make You Fall In Love with NYC Again." Jeremy Bender. <https://www.buzzfeed.com/jeremybender/hidden-gems-to-make-you-fall-in-love-with-nyc?utm_term=.atap4NDKl#.suxLe3qEo>

"9/11 Memorial and Museum." WTC. <https://en.wikipedia.org/wiki/National_September_11_Memorial_%26_Museum>

"About." NitehawkCinema.com. <http://www.nitehawkcinema.com/about-us/>

"About Chelsea Market." Chelsea Market.com. <http://chelseamarket.com/index.php/About/contact/about-chelsea-market>

"A Brief History of Orchard Street's Oldest Stores." Sarah Theeboom. <https://www.dnainfo.com/new-york/20161003/fort-greene/halloween-party-ideas-schedule-decorations-snacks-candy-games-for-kids-nyc>

"A Burial Ground and Its Dead Are Given Life." Edward Rothstein. <http://www.nytimes.com/2010/02/26/arts/design/26burial.html>

"A Guide to St. Patrick's Cathedral." NYC The Official Guide. <http://www.nycgo.com/articles/guide-to-st-patricks-cathedral>

"African Burial Ground National Monument." Wikipedia. <https://en.wikipedia.org/wiki/African_Burial_Ground_National_Monument>

"American Museum of Natural History." NYC The Official Guide. <http://www.nycgo.com/museums-galleries/american-museum-of-natural-history>

"American Museum of Natural History." Wikipedia. <https://en.wikipedia.org/wiki/American_Museum_of_Natural_History>

"Apollo Legends." Bio. <http://www.biography.com/people/groups/apollo-legends>

"Apollo Theater." NYC The Official Guide. <http://www.nycgo.com/venues/apollo-theater>

"Apollo Theater." Wikipedia. <https://en.wikipedia.org/wiki/Apollo_Theater>

"As a tourist what is the best area of New York to stay in?" Quora. <https://www.quora.com/As-a-tourist-what-is-the-best-area-of-New-York-to-stay-in>

"Astoria, Queens." Wikipedia. <https://en.wikipedia.org/wiki/Astoria,_Queens>

"Atlantic Avenue Subway Tunnel." James Maher. <https://www.jamesmaherphotography.com/new-york-historical-articles/atlantic-avenue-subway-tunnel/>

"Barclays Center." NYC The Official Guide. <http://www.nycgo.com/sports/barclays-center>

"Barclays Center." Wikipedia. <https://en.wikipedia.org/wiki/Barclays_Center>

"Battle of Long Island." Wikipedia. <https://en.wikipedia.org/wiki/Battle_of_Long_Island#Legacy>

"Bedford Avenue." Wikipedia. <https://en.wikipedia.org/wiki/Bedford_Avenue>

"Berlin Wall." Wikipedia. <https://en.wikipedia.org/wiki/Berlin_Wall#Fall_of_the_Wall>

"Best of the Lower East Side 2014: Shopping & Services." The Lo-Down. <http://www.thelodownny.com/leslog/2014/12/best-of-the-lower-east-side-2014-shopping-services.html>

"Blockhouse No. 1 (Central Park). Wikipedia. <https://en.wikipedia.org/wiki/Blockhouse_No._1_(Central_Park)>

"Broadway shows." NYC The Official Guide. <http://www.nycgo.com/broadway>

"Broadway theatre." Wikipedia. <https://en.wikipedia.org/wiki/Broadway_theatre>

"Bronx Zoo." Wikipedia. <https://en.wikipedia.org/wiki/Bronx_Zoo>

"Brooklyn." NYC The Official Guide. <http://www.nycgo.com/boroughs-neighborhoods/brooklyn>

"Brooklyn." Wikipedia. <https://en.m.wikipedia.org/wiki/Brooklyn>

"Brooklyn Botanic Garden." NYCGO. <http://www.nycgo.com/attractions/brooklyn-botanic-garden>

"Brooklyn Botanic Garden." Wikipedia. <https://en.wikipedia.org/wiki/Brooklyn_Botanic_Garden>

"Brooklyn Bowl." The Linq. <https://www.caesars.com/linq/promenade/things-to-do/brooklyn-bowl#.WBMY_LeKTIU>

"Brooklyn Bowl." Wikipedia. <https://en.wikipedia.org/wiki/Brooklyn_Bowl>

"Brooklyn Bridge." A View on Cities. <http://www.aviewoncities.com/nyc/brooklynbridge.htm>

"Brooklyn Bridge." Wikipedia. <https://en.wikipedia.org/wiki/Brooklyn_Bridge>

"Brooklyn Flea." Wikipedia. <https://en.wikipedia.org/wiki/Brooklyn_Flea>

"Brooklyn Market: Woodstock of Eating." Oliver Strand. <http://www.nytimes.com/2011/07/06/dining/reviews/smorgasburg-in-williamsburg-brooklyn-for-food-lovers.html?_r=0>

"Brooklyn, NY, borough guide." TimeOut. <https://www.timeout.com/newyork/brooklyn>

"Bryant Park." Wikipedia. <https://en.wikipedia.org/wiki/Bryant_Park>

"Bowery." Wikipedia. <https://en.wikipedia.org/wiki/Bowery#Bowery_Ballroom>

"Bowery Ballroom." Internet Archive WayBack Machine. <http://web.archive.org/web/20070718021919/http://www.boweryballroom.com/history.html>

"Bowery Ballroom." Wikipedia. <https://en.wikipedia.org/wiki/Bowery_Ballroom>

"Carnegie Hall." NYC-Arts. <http://www.nyc-arts.org/organizations/36/carnegie-hall>

"Carnegie Hall." NYC The Official Guide. <http://www.nycgo.com/venues/carnegie-hall>

"Carnegie Hall." Wikipedia. <https://en.wikipedia.org/wiki/Carnegie_Hall#Architecture>

"Castle Clinton." NPS. <https://www.nps.gov/cacl/learn/historyculture/index.htm>

"Castle Clinton." Wikipedia. <https://en.wikipedia.org/wiki/Castle_Clinton>

"Central Park. A View on Cities. <http://www.aviewoncities.com/nyc/centralpark.htm>

"Central Park." Wikipedia. <https://en.wikipedia.org/wiki/Central_Park>

"Chelsea." airbnb. <https://www.airbnb.com/locations/new-york/chelsea>

"Chelsea Historic District." Trust for Architectural Easements. <http://architecturaltrust.org/easements/about-the-trust/trust-protected-communities/historic-districts-in-new-york/chelsea-historic-district/>

"Chelsea, Manhattan." Wikipedia. <https://en.wikipedia.org/wiki/Chelsea,_Manhattan>

"Chelsea Market." Wikipedia. <https://en.wikipedia.org/wiki/Chelsea_Market>

"Chelsea, New York City." TripAdvisor. <https://www.tripadvisor.com/Neighborhood-g60763-n7102343-Chelsea-New_York_City_New_York.html>

"Chinatown, Manhattan." Wikipedia. <https://en.wikipedia.org/wiki/Chinatown,_Manhattan#Gentrification>

"Chinatown's "Bloody Angle" – A Trip Down Doyers Street." Nick Carr.

<http://www.huffingtonpost.com/nick-carr/chinatowns-bloody-angle_b_508118.html>

"Chrysler Building." New York Architecture. <http://www.nyc-architecture.com/MID/MID021.htm>

"Chrysler Building." Wikipedia. <https://en.wikipedia.org/wiki/Chrysler_Building>

"Chrysler Building Visitors Guide." About Travel. <http://gonyc.about.com/od/attractionslandmarks/p/chrysler_building.htm>

"City Hall (IRT Lexington Avenue Line)." Wikipedia. <https://en.wikipedia.org/wiki/City_Hall_(IRT_Lexington_Avenue_Line)>

"Coney Island." Wikipedia. <https://en.wikipedia.org/wiki/Coney_Island#Beach>

"Coney Island and Brighton Beach." Wikivoyage. <https://en.wikivoyage.org/wiki/Brooklyn/Coney_Island_and_Brighton_Beach>

"Discover something new at these boutique hotels in New York City." Savored Journeys. <http://www.savoredjourneys.com/2016/05/discover-something-new-boutique-hotels-new-york-city/>

"Doyers Street." Wikipedia. <https://en.wikipedia.org/wiki/Doyers_Street>

"Eat. Drink. Rock. Roll." Brooklyn Bowl. <http://www.brooklynbowl.com>

"Eating in Astoria, Queens: Restaurants, Cafés, Bakeries, and Markets." John Roleke. <http://queens.about.com/od/eatingout/a/eating_astoria.htm>

"Eldridge Street Synagogue." Wikipedia. <https://en.wikipedia.org/wiki/Eldridge_Street_Synagogue>

"Ellis Island." Wikipedia. <https://en.wikipedia.org/wiki/Ellis_Island#State_sovereignty_dispute>

"Ellis Island National Museum of Immigration." The Statue of Liberty – Ellis Island Foundation, Inc. <http://www.libertyellisfoundation.org/immigration-museum>

"Empire State Building." Wikipedia. <https://en.wikipedia.org/wiki/Empire_State_Building>

Empire State Building Experience." NYC The Official Guide. <http://www.nycgo.com/attractions/empire-state-building-experience>

"Fifth Avenue." A View on Cities. <http://www.aviewoncities.com/nyc/fifthavenue.htm>

"Fifth Avenue." Wikipedia. <https://en.wikipedia.org/wiki/Fifth_Avenue>

"Film Forum." Filmforum.org. <http://filmforum.org>

"Film Forum." Wikipedia. <https://en.wikipedia.org/wiki/Film_Forum>

"Flatiron District." Wikipedia. <https://en.wikipedia.org/wiki/Flatiron_District>

"Flatiron District, New York City." TripAdvisor. <https://www.tripadvisor.com/Neighborhood-g60763-n7102347-Flatiron_District-New_York_City_New_York.html>

"Frick Collection." Wikipedia. <https://en.wikipedia.org/wiki/Frick_Collection>

"Grand Central Terminal" NYC Tourist. <http://www.nyctourist.com/grandcentral1.htm>

"Grand Central Terminal." Wikipedia. <https://en.wikipedia.org/wiki/Grand_Central_Terminal>

"Greenwich Village." TripAdvisor. <https://www.tripadvisor.com/Neighborhood-g60763-n7102348-Greenwich_Village-New_York_City_New_York.html>

"Greenwich Village." Wikivoyage. <https://en.wikivoyage.org/wiki/Manhattan/Greenwich_Village>

"Greenwich Village." Wikipedia. <https://en.wikipedia.org/wiki/Greenwich_Village>

"Green-Wood Cemetery." Wikipedia. <https://en.wikipedia.org/wiki/Green-Wood_Cemetery>

"Hatchets and Blood: Scenes And Stories From The Deadliest Street In The United States." Nickolaus Hines. <http://all-that-is-interesting.com/bloody-angle>

"Hell Gate." Wikipedia. <https://en.wikipedia.org/wiki/Hell_Gate>

"Hell Gate Bridge." Wikipedia. <https://en.wikipedia.org/wiki/Hell_Gate_Bridge>

"Highlighting some of the Best Shopping and Dining Options in South Street Seaport and Pier 17." Ray Chin. <http://www.ahoynewyorkfoodtours.com/highlighting-some-of-the-best-shopping-and-dining-options-in-south-street-seaport-and-pier-17/>

"High Line (New York City)." Wikipedia. <https://en.wikipedia.org/wiki/High_Line_(New_York_City)>

"History of New York City." Wikipedia. <https://en.wikipedia.org/wiki/History_of_New_York_City>

"How to Choose Your NYC Hotel." NYCVP. <http://www.nyctrip.com/pages/Index.aspx?PageID=1466>

“How to Tour Old City Hall Station.” New York Transit Museum. <http://www.nytransitmuseum.org/oldcityhall/>

“How to Visit NYC’s Abandoned City Hall Subway Station.” Free Tours By Foot. <http://www.freetoursbyfoot.com/city-hall-subway-station/>

“How to Visit the Chrysler Building.” Peggy Epstein, studio. <http://traveltips.usatoday.com/visit-chrysler-building-12900.html>

“Inside NYC’s Stunning Ex-Subway Stop, Now ‘Open’ for Visitors.” Curbed.

"<http://ny.curbed.com/2014/2/14/10143642/inside-nycs-stunning-ex-subway-stop-now-open-for-visitors>

“Irish Hunger Memorial.” Atlas Obscura. <http://www.atlasobscura.com/places/irish-hunger-memorial>

“Irish Hunger Memorial.” Battery Park City Parks. <http://bpcparks.org/whats-here/parks/irish-hunger-memorial/>

"Irish Hunger Memorial." Wikipedia. <https://en.wikipedia.org/wiki/Irish_Hunger_Memorial>

"Ladies Lunch in NYC: Best Spots to Dine and Shop Along 5th Avenue." Guest of a Guest. <http://guestofaguest.com/new-york/restaurants/ladies-lunch-in-nyc-best-spots-to-dine-and-shop-along-5th-avenue>

"Ladies' Mile Historic District." Wikipedia. <https://en.wikipedia.org/wiki/Ladies%27_Mile_Historic_District>

"Lincoln Center for the Performing Arts." NYC-Arts. <http://www.nyc-arts.org/organizations/1767/lincoln-center-for-the-performing-arts>

"Lincoln Center for the Performing Arts." Wikipedia. <https://en.wikipedia.org/wiki/Lincoln_Center_for_the_Performing_Arts>

"List of Berlin Wall segments." Wikipedia. <https://en.wikipedia.org/wiki/List_of_Berlin_Wall_segments>

"Little Italy, Manhattan." Wikipedia. <https://en.wikipedia.org/wiki/Little_Italy,_Manhattan>

"Little Italy Restaurants and Other Things to See." Free Tours By Foot. <http://www.freetoursbyfoot.com/little-italy-restaurants-and-things-to-see/>

"Lower East Side." Airbnb. <https://www.airbnb.com/locations/new-york/lower-east-side>

"Lower East Side." Wikipedia. <https://en.wikipedia.org/wiki/Lower_East_Side>

"Lower East Side, New York City." TripAdvisor. <https://www.tripadvisor.com/Neighborhood-g60763-n7102351-Lower_East_Side-New_York_City_New_York.html>

"Lower East Side." Not for Tourists. <http://www.notfortourists.com/Hood.aspx/NewYork/LowerEastSide>

"Lower East Side Neighborhood Guide." TimeOut. <https://www.timeout.com/newyork/manhattan/lower-east-side-manhattan-neighborhood-guide>

"Lower East Side Tenement Museum." NPS. <https://www.nps.gov/loea/index.htm>

"Lower East Side Tenement Museum." Wikipedia. <https://en.wikipedia.org/wiki/Lower_East_Side_Tenement_Museum>

"Lower Manhattan." NYC The Official Guide. <http://www.nycgo.com/boroughs-neighborhoods/manhattan/lower-manhattan>

"Lower Manhattan." Wikipedia. <https://en.wikipedia.org/wiki/Lower_Manhattan>

"Macy's Herald Square." Wikipedia. <https://en.wikipedia.org/wiki/Macy%27s_Herald_Square>

"Macy's The World's Largest Store." NYC Tourist. <http://www.nyctourist.com/macys1.htm>

"Mad About Shopping." NYC The Official Guide. <http://www.nycgo.com/articles/mad-about-shopping-slideshow>

"Madame Tussauds New York." NYC The Official Guide. <http://www.nycgo.com/attractions/madame-tussauds-new-york>

"Madame Tussauds New York." Wikipedia. <https://en.wikipedia.org/wiki/Madame_Tussauds_New_York>

"Madison Avenue." Wikipedia. <https://en.wikipedia.org/wiki/Madison_Avenue>

"Madison Square Garden." NYCGO. <http://www.nycgo.com/attractions/madison-square-garden>

"Madison Square Garden." Wikipedia. <https://en.wikipedia.org/wiki/Madison_Square_Garden#Penn_Station_renovation_controversy>

"Mapping the 5 Pieces of the Berlin Wall in NYC." Untapped Cities. <http://untappedcities.com/2015/10/07/mapping-the-5-pieces-of-the-berlin-wall-in-nyc/?displayall=true>

"Metropolitan Museum of Art." NYC-Arts. <http://www.nyc-arts.org/organizations/4/metropolitan-museum-of-art>

"Metropolitan Museum of Art." Wikipedia. <https://en.wikipedia.org/wiki/Metropolitan_Museum_of_Art#History>

"Midtown Manhattan." Wikipedia. <https://en.wikipedia.org/wiki/Midtown_Manhattan>

"Midtown, New York City." TripAdvisor. <https://www.tripadvisor.com/Neighborhood-g60763-n7102352-Midtown-New_York_City_New_York.html>

"Morgan Library & Museum." Wikipedia. <https://en.wikipedia.org/wiki/Morgan_Library_%26_Museum>

"Museum of Modern Art." Wikipedia. <https://en.wikipedia.org/wiki/Museum_of_Modern_Art#53rd_Street_.281939.E2.80.93present.29>

"Museum of the City of New York." NYC The Official Guide. <http://www.nycgo.com/museums-galleries/museum-of-the-city-of-new-york>

“Museum of the City of New York.” Wikipedia. <https://en.wikipedia.org/wiki/Museum_of_the_City_of_New_York>

“Museums in New York City.” TripAdvisor. <https://www.tripadvisor.com.ph/Attractions-g60763-Activities-c49-New_York_City_New_York.html>

“Must-See Astoria.” Adam Kuban. <http://www.nycgo.com/articles/must-see-astoria-slideshow>

“Must-See Chinatown.” Michael Hsu. <http://www.nycgo.com/articles/must-see-chinatown-slideshow>

“Must-See NoLiTa and Little Italy.” Christopher Wallace. <http://www.nycgo.com/articles/must-see-nolita-little-italy-slideshow>

“National September 11 Memorial & Museum.” Wikipedia. <https://en.wikipedia.org/wiki/National_September_11_Memorial_%26_Museum>

"Neighborhoods." TripAdvisor. <https://www.tripadvisor.com/Travel-g60763-s204/New-York-City:New-York:Neighborhoods.html>

“New York City.” History.com. <http://www.history.com/topics/new-york-city>

“New York Night Tours.” Free Tours By Foot. <http://www.freetoursbyfoot.com/new-york-tours/night-tours/>

"New York City." Wikipedia. <https://en.m.wikipedia.org/wiki/New_York_City>

“New York City: 10 Things to Do.” Joe Angio. <http://content.time.com/time/travel/cityguide/article/0,31489,1843404_1843415_1843479,00.html>

“New York City’s 25 Most Iconic Pizzerias.” Greg Morabito. <http://ny.eater.com/maps/new-york-citys-25-most-iconic-pizzerias>

“New York-style Pizza.” Wikipedia. <https://en.wikipedia.org/wiki/New_York-style_pizza>

“Nitehawk Cinema.” NYMag. <http://nymag.com/listings/bar/nitehawk-cinema/>

“Nitehawk Cinema.” Village Voice. <http://www.villagevoice.com/location/nitehawk-cinema-6455256>

“Nolita.” Wikipedia. <https://en.wikipedia.org/wiki/Nolita>

“Welcome to Chinatown.” New York Chinatown. <http://new-york-chinatown.info>

“New York City Neighborhoods.” Frommer’s. <http://www.frommers.com/destinations/new-york-city/663739>

“New York Public Library.” Wikipedia. <https://en.wikipedia.org/wiki/New_York_Public_Library>

“New York Public Library Main Branch.” Wikipedia. <https://en.wikipedia.org/wiki/New_York_Public_Library_Main_Branch>

“Orchard Street Gets Even More Appetizing With These 18 New Restaurants.” Mary Jane Weedman. <http://www.grubstreet.com/2013/10/new-restaurants-orchard-street.html>

“Orchard Street (Manhattan).” Wikipedia. <https://en.wikipedia.org/wiki/Orchard_Street_(Manhattan)>

"Queens." NYC The Official Guide. <http://www.nycgo.com/boroughs-neighborhoods/queens>

"Queens." Wikipedia. <https://en.m.wikipedia.org/wiki/Queens>

“Radio City Music Hall.” About Travel. <http://manhattan.about.com/od/historyandlandmarks/a/rockefellercent_3.htm>

“Radio City Music Hall.” Wikipedia. <https://en.wikipedia.org/wiki/Radio_City_Music_Hall>

"Radio City Music Hall." Yelp. <https://www.yelp.com/biz/radio-city-music-hall-new-york-4>

"Return of a Long-Dormant Island of Grace." Edward Rothstein. <http://www.nytimes.com/2007/12/01/arts/design/01eldr.html>

"Rockefeller Center NYC. NYC Tourist. <http://www.nyctourist.com/rock_center1.htm>

"Rockefeller Center." Wikipedia. <https://en.wikipedia.org/wiki/Rockefeller_Center>

"Secrets of the Cloisters." NewYork.com. <http://www.newyork.com/articles/attractions/the-secrets-of-the-cloisters-67067/>

"Secrets of Green-Wood cemetery: Famous Residents, Civil War connections, and more." Brian Levinson. <http://www.amny.com/secrets-of-new-york/secrets-of-green-wood-cemetery-famous-residents-civil-war-connections-more-1.11470772>

"Shopping Along 5th Avenue." NYC Tourist. <http://www.nyctourist.com/shopping_fifthave.htm>

"Shopping Along Madison Avenue." NYC Tourist. <http://www.nyctourist.com/shopping_madisonave.htm>

"Smallpox Hospital." Wikipedia. <https://en.wikipedia.org/wiki/Smallpox_Hospital>

"Smallpox Hospital, Roosevelt Island." The New York Landmarks Conservatory. <http://www.nylandmarks.org/programs_services/technical_assistance/projects/smallpox_hospital_roosevelt_island/>

"SoHo-Cast Iron Historic District." The New York Preservation Archive Project. <http://www.nypap.org/preservation-history/soho-cast-iron-historic-district/>

"SoHo, Manhattan." Wikipedia. <https://en.wikipedia.org/wiki/SoHo,_Manhattan>

"SoHo, New York City Travel Guide." Oyster.com. <https://www.oyster.com/new-york-city/areas/soho/>

"South Street Seaport." A View on Cities. <http://www.aviewoncities.com/nyc/southstreetseaport.htm>

"South Street Seaport." Wikipedia. <https://en.wikipedia.org/wiki/South_Street_Seaport>

"St. Patrick's Cathedral (Manhattan)." Wikipedia. <https://en.wikipedia.org/wiki/St._Patrick%27s_Cathedral_(Manhattan)>

"Staten Island boat graveyard." Wikipedia. <https://en.wikipedia.org/wiki/Staten_Island_boat_graveyard>

"Staten Island Ferry." NYCGO. <http://www.nycgo.com/attractions/staten-island-ferry>

"Staten Island Ferry." Wikipedia. <https://en.wikipedia.org/wiki/Staten_Island_Ferry>

"Statue of Liberty." UNESCO. <http://whc.unesco.org/en/list/307>

"Statue of Liberty." Wikipedia. <https://en.wikipedia.org/wiki/Statue_of_Liberty>

"Surveying Williamsburg's Bedford Avenue, now approaching peak post-gentrification." Amy Plitt. <http://ny.curbed.com/2016/8/1/12342638/bedford-avenue-williamsburg-brooklyn-gentrification>

"Ten Tips for New York Tourists." Liz Humphreys and Special to USA Today. <http://abcnews.go.com/Travel/Vacation/story?id=4282010&page=1>

"The 10 Best Pizzas in NYC." Zachary Feldman. <http://www.villagevoice.com/restaurants/the-10-best-pizzas-in-nyc-6531467>

"The 15 Best Museums in New York City." Foursquare Lists. <https://foursquare.com/top-places/new-york-city/best-places-museums>

"The 25 Best Bars in NYC Right Now." Chris Schonberger. <http://firstwefeast.com/drink/best-bars-in-nyc-right-now/>

"The Absolute Best Dance Club in New York." Lauren Schwartzberg. <http://www.grubstreet.com/bestofnewyork/best-clubs-in-nyc.html>

"The Atlantic Avenue Tunnel." The Brooklyn Historic Railway Association. <http://www.brooklynrail.net/proj_aatunnel.html>

"The Best 10 Shopping near 12 Fulton Street, New York, NY." Yelp. <https://www.yelp.com/search?cflt=shopping&find_loc=South+Street+Seaport%2C+Manhattan%2C+NY>

"The Best East Village Eateries." Kaitlin Menza. <http://www.refinery29.com/east-village-restaurants#slide-1>

"The best East village restaurants in NYC." TimeOut.com. <https://www.timeout.com/newyork/restaurants/east-village-restaurant-guide?package_page=35599>

"The best flea markets in NYC." TimeOut.com. <https://www.timeout.com/newyork/shopping/best-flea-markets>

"The best Lower East Side restaurants." Christina Izzo and Time Out contributors. <https://www.timeout.com/newyork/restaurants/best-restaurants-lower-east-side?package_page=35599>

"The best Williamsburg restaurants." Christina Izzo." TimeOut. <https://www.timeout.com/newyork/restaurants/williamsburg-restaurant-guide?package_page=35599>

"The Big 5: Most-Visited Museums in NYC." NYC The Official Guide. <http://www.nycgo.com/articles/the-big-5-most-visited-museums-in-nyc>

"The Blockhouse and the Bench." Forgotten New York. <http://forgotten-ny.com/2001/03/the-blockhouse-and-the-bench/>

"The "bloody angle" of Chinatown's Doyers Street." Ephemeral New York. <https://ephemeralnewyork.wordpress.com/2011/07/04/the-bloody-angle-of-chinatowns-doyers-street/>

"The Bowery Presents." Wikipedia. <https://en.wikipedia.org/wiki/The_Bowery_Presents>

"The Brooklyn Bridge." History.com. <http://www.history.com/topics/brooklyn-bridge>

"The Childhood of a Renowned President." NPS. <https://www.nps.gov/thrb/index.htm>

"The Cloisters." Wikipedia. <https://en.wikipedia.org/wiki/The_Cloisters>

"The Cloisters: NYC Day-Trip Getaway." Huffington Post. <http://www.huffingtonpost.com/2010/09/16/spend-a-day-in-nyc-the-cl_n_717837.html>

"The Five Places to See Pieces of the Berlin Wall in NYC." Matt Coneybeare. <https://viewing.nyc/the-five-places-to-see-pieces-of-the-berlin-wall-in-nyc/>

"The Frick Collection." Google Arts & Culture. <https://www.google.com/culturalinstitute/beta/partner/the-frick-collection>

"The Morgan Library & Museum." NYC The Official Guide. <http://www.nycgo.com/museums-galleries/the-morgan-library-museum>

"Theodore Roosevelt." Wikipedia. <https://en.wikipedia.org/wiki/Theodore_Roosevelt>

"Theodore Roosevelt Birthplace National Historic Site." Wikipedia. <https://en.wikipedia.org/wiki/Theodore_Roosevelt_Birthplace_National_Historic_Site>

"The Roosevelt Family Houses in NYC and New York State." Jackie Spear.

<http://untappedcities.com/2016/05/05/roosevelt-family-houses-new-york-city/>

"The Staten Island Ferry." Siferry.com. <http://www.siferry.com>

"The Strange History of NYC's Mighty Hell Gate." Ryan Healy. <http://gothamist.com/2016/02/22/hell_gate_history_nyc.php>

"The Times Square, New York guide." Jennifer Picht and Time Out contributors. <https://www.timeout.com/newyork/things-to-do/new-york-attractions-times-square>

"Things to See in Chinatown New York: A Self Guided Tour." Free Tours By Foot. <http://www.freetoursbyfoot.com/things-to-see-in-chinatown-new-york-a-self-guided-tour/>

"Times Square." Wikipedia. <https://en.wikipedia.org/wiki/Times_Square>

"To 25 Ways to Save on New York City Travel." Independent Traveler.com. <http://www.independenttraveler.com/travel-tips/mid-atlantic/top-25-ways-to-save-on-new-york-city-travel>

Trinity Church (Manhattan)." Wikipedia. <https://en.wikipedia.org/wiki/Trinity_Church_(Manhattan)#Burial_grounds>

"Trinity Church Cemetery." Wikipedia. <https://en.wikipedia.org/wiki/Trinity_Church_Cemetery>

"Trinity Churchyard." Atlas Obscura. <http://www.atlasobscura.com/places/trinity-churchyard>

"Tugboat Graveyard." Atlas Obscura. <http://www.atlasobscura.com/places/tugboat-graveyard>

"Upper East Side." NYC The Official Guide. <http://www.nycgo.com/boroughs-neighborhoods/manhattan/upper-east-side>

"Upper East Side." Wikipedia. <https://en.wikipedia.org/wiki/Upper_East_Side>

"Upper West Side." NYC The Official Guide. <http://www.nycgo.com/boroughs-neighborhoods/manhattan/upper-west-side>

"Upper West Side." Wikipedia. <https://en.wikipedia.org/wiki/Upper_West_Side>

"Visiting Ellis Island." The Statue of Liberty – Ellis Island Foundation, Inc. <http://www.libertyellisfoundation.org/visiting-ellis-island>

"Wall Street." A View on Cities. <http://www.aviewoncities.com/nyc/wallstreet.htm>

"Wall Street." Wikipedia. <https://en.wikipedia.org/wiki/Wall_Street>

"Wall Street Tour." Wall Street Walks. <https://wallstreetwalks.com>

"Washington Square." A View on Cities. <http://www.aviewoncities.com/nyc/washingtonsquare.htm>

"Washington Square Park." Wikipedia. <https://en.wikipedia.org/wiki/Washington_Square_Park>

"What's So Special About Broadway?" Wonderpolis. <http://wonderopolis.org/wonder/whats-so-special-about-broadway/>

"Where to Stay." NYC.com. <http://www.nyc.com/visitor_guide/where_to_stay.75912/amp/>

"Why Can't I Dance? – NYC's Cabaret Laws." TripAdvisor. <https://www.tripadvisor.com.ph/ShowTopic-g60763-i5-k4094248-Why_Can_t_I_Dance_NYC_s_Cabaret_Laws-New_York_City_New_York.html>

"Yankee Stadium." Ballparks of Baseball.com. <http://www.ballparksofbaseball.com/ballparks/yankee-stadium/>

"Yankee Stadium." Wikipedia. <https://en.wikipedia.org/wiki/Yankee_Stadium>

"You Can Come and Go. They're Staying Awhile. Seth Kugel. <http://www.nytimes.com/2008/11/30/travel/30weekend.html?_r=0>

Feeding Baby
Cynthia Cherry
978-1941070000

Axolotl
Lolly Brown
978-0989658430

Dysautonomia, POTS Syndrome
Frederick Earlstein
978-0989658485

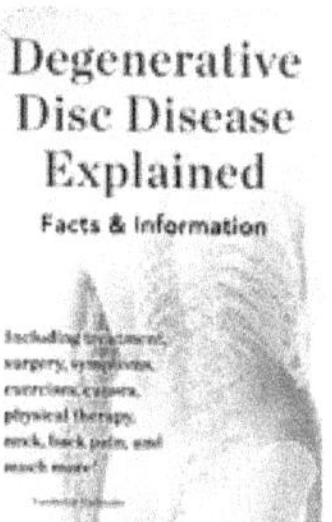

Degenerative Disc Disease Explained
Frederick Earlstein
978-0989658485

Sinusitis, Hay Fever,
Allergic Rhinitis Explained
Frederick Earlstein
978-1941070024

Wicca
Riley Star
978-1941070130

Zombie Apocalypse
Rex Cutty
978-1941070154

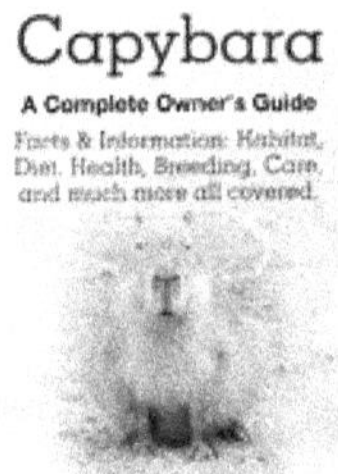

Capybara
Lolly Brown
978-1941070062

Eels As Pets
Lolly Brown
978-1941070167

Scabies and Lice Explained
Frederick Earlstein
978-1941070017

Saltwater Fish As Pets
Lolly Brown
978-0989658461

Torticollis Explained
Frederick Earlstein
978-1941070055

Kennel Cough
Lolly Brown
978-0989658409

Physiotherapist, Physical Therapist
A Career Guide

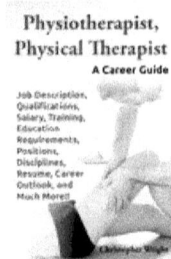

Physiotherapist, Physical Therapist
Christopher Wright
978-0989658492

Rats, Mice, and Dormice As Pets
The Complete Owner's Guide

Rats, Mice, and Dormice As Pets
Lolly Brown
978-1941070079

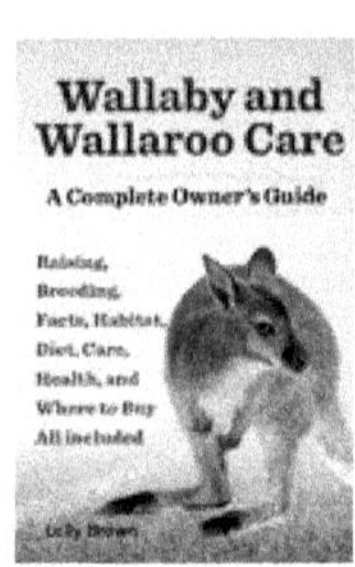

Wallaby and Wallaroo Care
Lolly Brown
978-1941070031

Bodybuilding Supplements
Explained
Jon Shelton
978-1941070239

Demonology
Riley Star
978-19401070314

Pigeon Racing
Lolly Brown
978-1941070307

Dwarf Hamster
Lolly Brown
978-1941070390

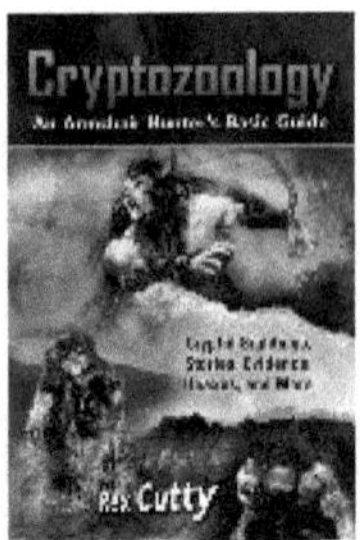

Cryptozoology
Rex Cutty
978-1941070406

Eye Strain
Frederick Earlstein
978-1941070369

Inez The Miniature Elephant
Asher Ray
978-1941070353

Vampire Apocalypse
Rex Cutty
978-1941070321

www.ingramcontent.com/pod-product-compliance
Lightning Source LLC
Chambersburg PA
CBHW051950090426
42741CB00008B/1340

9781941070956